Picasso and Marie-Thérèse Walter, 1925-1927

Herbert T. Schwarz

Éditions Isabeau Inc.

Picasso and Marie-Thérèse Walter, 1925-1927.
Herbert T. Schwarz
Copyright © 1988 by Éditions Isabeau Inc..
Copyright © Pablo Picasso 1988 — Vis-Art Copyright Inc.

ISBN 0-9693407-0-2
Schwarz, Herbert, 1921—

Published in Canada by Éditions Isabeau Inc.
Head office: Inuvik, N.W.T. Canada

Postal adress and distribution:
P.O.Box 364
Sillery, Québec
Canada G1P 2R5

Cover illustration *The Seated Girl*, 1926.

Printed and bound in Montmagny, Qué. by Les Éditions Marquis Ltée, in May 1988.

to Marie-Thérèse Walter

Preface

I hear from afar, disrupting the ageless silence, bells ringing, dogs yelping. A human voice joins in the cry. A dog-team appears on the horizon, briskly pulling Joe Avik's heavily laden sled with wide-eyed kids on top. Trotting behind, a group of Eskimos laughing and shouting . They pass by my cabin, cross the ice-bound Kugmalit Bay, and, now on the snowy tundra, smaller and smaller, disappear on the horizon.

I look at them and wonder what my Eskimo friend would say if I were to tell him the story of Picasso and Marie-Thérèse Walter? I have no doubt that I would offend his Eskimo sense of propriety. Surprised, he would turn at me bluntly: "But why all this fuss? Why are you telling me this? That clever old man and the young girl were only doing their own thing, which is none of your business, none of your concern!"

His wisdom, born out of millenia of hardships and philosophical acceptance of things, is truer than mine. I know it, but I am not at peace, because in this brooding silence I am relentlessly haunted by the demon of Picasso's sketch.

It is the portrait of a fair young girl, a mere teenager in a cheap striped dress, tensed and ill at ease, gravely trying to disclose a secret.

But what could this teen-ager's secret be?

With our eyes clear, let us plunge into this Picassian adventure and look at it.

H.T.S.

Tuktoyaktuk on the Arctic Ocean.
North West Territories
Canada.

Carl Jung's synchronicity relating to the study: "Picasso and Marie-Thérèse Walter, 1925-1927"

If it were not for a number of some of the most remarkable coincidences, chance happenings and encounters, expressed by Carl Jung's term *synchronicity*, this study of Picasso's early relationship with Marie-Thérèse would have never taken place.

It had the most unlikely beginning...

In May 1940, at the time the German army was advancing towards Paris, the great collection of the Parisian art dealer and connoisseur Ambroise Vollard, comprising numerous works by Cézanne, Degas, Rouault, Bonnard, Redon, Gauguin and Renoir (36!) as well as one blue-period Picasso, was hastily dispatched to Spain and then to Portugal, and from there shipped on a neutral vessel to the United States for safekeeping.

Off the coast of Bermuda, this vessel was intercepted by the Royal Navy, and on suspicion that the paintings had been stolen by the Germans, the collection was seized and stored for the duration of the war at the National Gallery of Canada in Ottawa. After the war, it was repossessed by Vollard's heirs. Eventually, the blue period Picasso *Femme Assise* 1903, was acquired by an acquaintance of mine in Canada. The painting was not signed, but it was based on Picasso's Barcelona sketches, and it was executed in a masterly fashion. Also, in view of Vollard's worldwide reputation, was readily accepted by art historians and experts as a genuine blue-period Picasso. In years to come *Femme Assise* would be exhibited in Canada and France, and finally shown at a prestigious Picasso retrospective.

a

It happened, however, that to everybody's amazement Picasso, on receiving the catalogue from this retrospective, pronounced this blue period Picasso, not his! When pressed for details he reluctantly admitted that it was brought to him in the early thirties by a Catalan friend, together with three other paintings done in his blue-period style, but he refused to divulge his friend's identity. "A month or so later", said Picasso, "I saw the four paintings in the most prominent Parisian galleries, including Vollard's, and told them the paintings were not mine".[*]

And there the matter rested for a number of years. Meanwhile, a personal fascination I had with Picasso was becoming an obsession. I met and talked to a number of his close friends and associates in France and Spain, and also tried to discover the identity of that mysterious painter who had so skillfully interpreted Picasso's Barcelona sketches for *Femme Assise.*

In 1966, the owner of *Femme Assise* entrusted the case to the Parisian lawyer, Roland Dumas, to find out what he could about this painting's origin. Dumas took the painting directly to Picasso, who did not offer him any additional information, and once more asserted his previously stated opinion, the painting was not his.

In 1972, I received information to the effect that a Catalan artist had visited Picasso at his Boisgeloup Château in March-April 1933, when Marie-Thérèse, Picasso's mistress, was also known to have been there.

I encountered Marie-Thérèse in Menton in 1974. Our discussion did not touch on her personal life, which was already documented in great detail. If there was a mystery to be solved, it did not involve Marie-Thérèse, but *Femme Assise* and its unknown artist.

---

[*]   *That Unknown Picasso*, text Herbert T. SCHWARZ, photography, André VILLERS, submitted for publication.

At the time of our meeting Marie-Thérèse was leading a lonely existence, but she was a warm and gracious hostess. After trying to answer some of my queries, she not unexpectedly delved into the past, and that great "amour fou" with Picasso. Her past was Picasso's past and to prove it she showed me photos, many of them taken by Picasso, as well as precious letters and souvenirs.

This meeting took place not quite one year after Picasso's death in April 1973, but Marie-Thérèse seemed cheerful enough and talked of the villa in Juan-les-Pins that she would soon inhabit, of its large garden, and of space for her pet doves...

Only later, with perspective of time, did I realize to what extent I had been affected by this meeting, and only recently was I able to comprehend Marie-Thérèse's startled expression during our introduction. I had frequently talked of her with Ines Sassier, Picasso's confidante and housekeeper in Paris during the last war, who was very fond of Marie-Thérèse and knew her well.

In the Fall of 1977, I received news that Marie-Thérèse Léontide Deslorier Walter hanged herself on the 19th of October in her villa at Juan-les-Pins.

In 1979, at Saint-Paul-de-Vence, I met quite by chance a man who told me of a strange conversation that he had had with Marie-Thérèse shortly before her death. But only later did I realize the possible significance of what he told me for the story of her relationship with Picasso.

In April 1983, on the tenth anniversary of Picasso's death, I traveled to Vallauris, Mougins, and Vauvenargues where Picasso had once worked and lived, and at Mougins I encountered Jacqueline Picasso, still a recluse in those days. She was most decidedly not an easy person to see, but somehow a remarkable friendship developed from this totally unexpected meeting, a friendship which brought to fruition my folio, *Hommage à Picasso* that year, and in May 1985 the

Montréal Picasso exhibition of works from Jacqueline Picasso's collection. Inspired by this prestigious exhibition, Montréal art dealers vied with each other to stock their galleries to overflowing with Picassos. It happened that on 8 April 1986 I visited a prestigious art gallery in Montréal and was shown Picasso's pen and ink sketch, *The Seated Girl..* It was already in the process of being crated...

The subject of the *Seated Girl* seemed such an obvious likeness to the young Marie-Thérèse! The prominent nose, the winged hair, the grave facial expression, and that "col Claudine" and striped dress, her famous trademark. But there was something very unusual about this sketch, its date: "1926". By Picasso's own admission he did not know Marie-Thérèse until January 1927!

The following morning, as *Seated Girl* was landing in London, I was deep in a study of Picasso's early relationship with Marie-Thérèse. Contrary to my expectations there were few clues to follow. Nevertheless, in the hectic months that followed, the pieces of this Picassian puzzle slowly fell into place. However, a major riddle remained unsolved.

It centered around one of Picasso's most important paintings, *L'Atelier de la Modiste* 1926 in which the young Marie-Thérèse, still before January 1927, seemed to figure. The painting did not reflect Picasso's autobiographical tendencies, which I had observed during months of arduous work, and thus weakened the credibility of my study. This, of course, bothered me as I was convinced that in this major painting Picasso was describing an event which for him had an extraordinary significance. But what was it?

I assumed that Picasso was portraying a factual event which centered around Marie-Thérèse, and that this assumption, if proven correct would not only confirm my earlier work, but may also provide me with the totally unknown details concerning her life before meeting Picasso.

d

With this supposition in mind I proceeded to France to search for Picasso's mysterious *Atelier de la Modiste*, but had no success.

Fruitless though the search was, it led me to the villa at Maisons Alfort, where Marie-Thérèse had lived with her mother, Émilie Marguerite, more than 60 years ago.

The villa, unoccupied and decaying, remains to this day part of the Walter estate, no less than 11 claimants fight for a share in it. It was at this juncture in my inquiry that I was confronted with an extraordinary coincidence. At one time Marie-Thérèse's mother had been married to a namesake of mine, and I was taken for a potential claimant! This I denied, but nevertheless, I obtained meaningful clues for the extension of my search, as well as one vital piece of information, which, however, I put aside, as I had made arrangements to visit Jacqueline Picasso at Mougins prior to her departure for Barcelona. But again fate intervened and swept me into an altogether different direction, which shortly afterwards, led me to the most dramatic event in this story.

An unexpected tragedy, a totally incomprehensible event, prevented me from keeping my engagement. On the 15th of October 1986, Jacqueline Picasso killed herself.

Saddened and bewildered by this repetition of Picassian tragedy, at loss as to what to do next, I stayed on in Paris, and once more, began gathering time-worn threads that lead me back to Émilie Marguerite Walter, Marie-Thérèse, and that mysterious Atelier...

Only three days after the tragedy at Notre-Dame-de-Vie, acting on the information that I had received, I left Paris and drove eastwards to a famous wine growing region; the narrow country lane passed terraced vineyards, and gently rolling hills, until at journey's end, the road ascended steeply to a house, which, at the top of a hill, held a commanding view of the valley. A tall, animated lady with heavy greyish hair, finely chiseled features, and the most beautiful searching eyes emerged from the house to welcome me.

At first this meeting seemed almost unbelievable, for as I greeted the woman, I was coming to the end of a long and amazing journey, packed with surprises and truly remarkable happenings; standing in front of me was Marie-Thérèse's sister!

Hardly anything is known of her, yet this woman figures in many of Picasso's finest paintings. Her's was a special closeness and deep affection for the younger Marie-Thérèse, and for many years the two beautiful sisters were inseparable. This woman holds a wealth of warm recollections, and my story is also her's. Because when a world famous artist was following a blonde girl to Gare St.Lazare, she was there.

f

On Boulevard Haussman in front of the Galeries Lafayette department store, o n January 8th 1927, I noticed a pretty blonde girl, and looked at her, and looked at her.
I followed her, accosted, spoke:

"Miss, you've an interesting face. I would like to do your portrait. I am Picasso."

My name meant nothing to her.

Two days later I met her again at the appointed place in Gare St.Lazare: "Miss, we'll do great things together".
So I took this girl to the nearest bookstore to find a book telling her something about me. They had only one, and it was in Japanese.

Picasso

Picasso and Marie-Thérèse Walter

1925-1927

Part 1

Canada

Picasso's fireside armchair.

In September 1909, after five years of precarious existence, Picasso, now backed by some wealthy collectors and avant-garde dealers, abandons his old den at the Bateau Lavoir and with Fernande Olivier, moves into more adequate quarters at 11 Boulevard de Clichy. There, as befits an artist on the road to fame, he acquires a white-aproned maid to look after the *ménage*. His only too recent privations are not that readily forgotten, however; he and Fernande haunt *brocanteurs* and junk shops and buy all kinds of second-hand furniture. According to Fernande[1], the furniture is not attractive. It is heavy and cumbersome, but functional enough to satisfy Picasso who never bothers much about such trivial matters.

On one of their expeditions Picasso acquires a "fireside armchair," since fireplaces are the main source of heating for most Parisian apartments. Perhaps it is kept in the apartment, perhaps it is moved to the Bateau Lavoir, where Picasso rents another studio in order to work in the isolation he craves. In any case, from 1909 to 1932 Picasso, that faithful chronicler of his own life, will portray this chair in a multiplicity of drawings, sketches, and oils; it is the background for portraits of models, friends, wife, mistresses. Throughout this period, although the armchair undergoes Picasso's stylistic interpretations or changes in colour, it is clearly recognizable, even in his most fragmented cubist phase (Fig.1).

---

1   Fernande OLIVIER, *Picasso and his friends*, London, Heineman, 1964.

Fig.1   *Woman in a Chemise in an Armchair*, oil on canvas,
Paris, 1913.

Later when Picasso's work becomes more representational, the chair continues to be portrayed according to Picasso's deep-rooted feelings towards his subject. The chair becomes convulsively elongated and red when his screaming wife, Olga, sits in it (Fig.2). It expands assuming a curvilinear, pinkish, glowing aspect around the voluptuous body of Marie-Thérèse (Fig.3).

This is an ugly chair, although it will not appear so in Picasso's pictures. Heavy, plush, high-backed, with thick sausage-padded armrests, somewhat splayed, and sides reaching almost to the middle of the seat, it is very deep and probably covered by a thick cushion. It rests on two short, bulbous legs in front, and on two straight ones in back; all are at times obscured by a stringy drapery.

It would seem that, for a time after Picasso's marriage to Olga in 1918, and their move from the Hôtel Lutetia to 23 rue la Boétie, Picasso's simple furniture, including his bulky armchair, had to do. Picasso's drawing of *Olga's Salon* in 1919[2], is almost a caricature of his life with her; veritable lady of the manor, Olga sits enthroned in the chair, but only part of it is visible, because most is hidden by her enormous fur stole wrap. Sitting around her, stiff and uncomfortable, are three solemn young men: Jean Cocteau, Eric Satie, and Clive Bell.

What a far cry is this from Picasso's gay bohemian days! Not long after the socially ambitious Olga acquires white period pieces to suit her refined taste. Picasso's old armchair, the one which in the past had supported Fernande Olivier, Eva Humbert, the shadowy Marguerite Pichot, "the hero" Apollinaire (his head swathed in bandages), and the now estranged Max Jacob, the one which had formed the backdrop for some of Picasso's finest cubist paintings, is relegated to his studio at the top of the building, where complete chaos

---

2   Not illustrated in Zervos

Fig.2   *Nude in an Armchair*, oil on canvas, Paris, May 1929.

Fig.3 *The Dream*, January 1932.

and squalor reigned undisturbed. Very few of Picasso's close friends ever visit this studio[3]; Olga is not allowed in.[4]

---

[3] G. BRASSAI, *The Artists in my life*, London, Thames and Hudson, 1942, p.156. In 1932 Brassai visited Picasso's studio at 23 rue La Boétie, and remarked that it was devoid of furniture. By then Picasso's armchair was at Boisgeloup.

[4] For a time Picasso allowed Olga and the cleaning woman to enter his Studio every 2 weeks, but in later years these visits were disallowed.

Sketch of The Seated Girl, 1926.

In April 1986, I had an opportunity to examine in detail a pen-and-ink sketch by Picasso of a teen-age girl sitting in his bulky armchair[5] (Fig.4), the same that had appeared regularly in his works since 1909. This time, however, it was not the chair that attracted my attention, but the girl. She appears self-conscious, ill at ease. Her startled eyes convey inner tension and gravity. A prominent nose almost dissects her high forehead, embraced on each side by a winged sweep of blonde hair. She is wearing a striped dress with a broad rectangular Peter Pan collar (a "col Claudine," named after the heroine of Collette's novel) and is holding an open book or sketch-book on her lap.

What made this sketch so interesting was its striking resemblance to Marie-Thérèse Walter in photos of her as a teenager (Photo 1, Maya Ruiz Widmaier Picasso coll.) and in early pencil sketches by Picasso still in existence. The very image Picasso would be painting in 1927, but the sketch was dated 1926! The work had an impeccable pedigree: Henri Kahnweiler, Justin Thannhauser, Guggenheim Museum, New York, and an exhibition in Zurich, Switzerland in 1932.

Marie-Thérèse Walter was born in July 1909. It has been assumed by many art historians and experts that Picasso prefigured her several years before their meeting, but the date of that meeting was for

---

5   Courtesy Mark London, Elca London Gallery, Montréal.

11

Fig.4   *The Seated Girl*, pen and ink, 1926.

Photo 1 Marie-Thérèse Walter, as a teen-ager.
Collection Maya Ruiz Picasso.

a time shrouded in mystery. Patrick O'Brian[6], in 1956, remarked that "the season and even the year is uncertain."   The following year Antonina Vallentin assumed that the event took place "around 1931"[7]. Finally Picasso himself revealed to Françoise Gilot[8] that "this meeting took place on the 8th of January 1927 in front of the Lafayette store in Paris." And this date was subsequently confirmed by Marie-Thérèse herself.

---

6   Patrick O'BRIAN, *Picasso*, New York, G.P. Putman's Sons, 1956.

7   Antonina VALLENTIN, *Picasso*, Paris, Albin Michel, 1957.

8   Françoise GILOT, Carlton LAKE, *Life with Picasso*, New York, New American Library, 1965, p. 160

Picasso's "Sculptural Sketches," 1926.

The same year that Picasso sketched *The Seated Girl*, he did five other sketches of girls' faces, four of which are reproduced here in Fig.5. All bear a remarkable similarity to the face in *The Seated Girl* (Fig.4). In them Picasso apparently prefigured Marie-Thérèse's classic Nordic face: her fairness, her winged hair, and especially her nose, that prominent nose, which seems to invade most of her forehead, and which held him as under a spell. In Fig.5a, and b, it has such a plastic and sculptural aspect, that it might easily have served him as a model for his Boisgeloup sculptures and paintings of Marie-Thérèse in the thirties!

The sketch in Fig.5 c dated 20 March 1926 has some peculiar features. Within the girl's face is the profile of another face, a man's, sharper, more angular; the neck of the man is formed by the girl's black Peter Pan collar, which extends into an arm drawing the girl's face to him. Again, in Fig.5 c and d is the Peter Pan collar and the striped dress found in *The Seated Girl*.

Thus, if the sketch of 20 March 1926 was a representation of Marie-Thérèse, it preceded her meeting with Picasso by almost a year. The meaning of the profile within the girl's face, also observed in Picasso's sketch of *The Seated Girl* (Fig.4), was obscure. I will refer to it again.

Fig.5   "Sculptural Sketches," *Tête de Femme*, 1926.

a

b

c

d

Observations of Brydon Smith, Vivian Barnett, and Pierre Daix.

In 1967 Brydon Smith[9] observed that *The Seated Girl* (Fig.4) was closely related to *The Seated Woman*, grisaille in the Art Gallery of Ontario (Fig.23). The latter was dated 1926-1927, and this was significant since Picasso had acknowledged meeting Marie-Thérèse early in January 1927.

In her description, "The Thannhauser at the Guggenheim's" exhibition in 1978, Vivian Barnett[10] endorsed Brydon Smith's analysis, and extended it to another *Seated Woman*, circa 1927, an oil on wood in the Museum of Modern Art (Z-VII-77), and to *l'Atelier de la Modiste*, Jan. 1926, a grisaille in the Musée National d'Art Moderne, Paris (Fig.50).

In 1983 Pierre Daix[11] published a paper on his discovery of a "hidden portrait" of Marie-Thérèse in *The Still Life with Musical Instruments, circa* 1925 (Z-V-416), and this study posed a number of difficulties since Marie-Thérèse apparently had not entered Picasso's

---

9   Brydon SMITH, "Contemporary Canadian Art: Arts in Canada", *Arts Canada*, 3 March 1967, p.11-16

10   Vivian BARNETT, *Catalogue: The Guggenheim Museum: Justin K. Thannhauser Collection*, 1978.

11   Pierre DAIX, "On the Hidden Portrait of Marie-Thérèse" *American Arts*, Sept. 1983, p.125-128

life until January 1927. Daix's observations will be discussed later in this paper.

Observations of Lydia Gasman and
John Richardson.

In pursuing my study of *The Seated Girl*, 1926, and its possible connection to Marie-Thérèse, I came across a puzzling suggestion by John Richardson, who quoted extensively from interviews of Marie-Thérèse by Lydia Gasman[12] in 1971-1972:

> "The portrait drawings of Marie-Thérèse that Picasso was known to have done when he first met her, have disappeared, destroyed apparently, because the model had to hide them from her mother and the artist from his wife."[13]

For Picasso the hoarder, who never threw anything away, to have destroyed these portraits on account of Olga would have been unthinkable. He could have secreted them safely in his studio, which Olga was not allowed to enter. Moreover, he showed utter disregard for Olga when he exhibited paintings of Marie-Thérèse at the Gallery Georges Petit in 1932, but that of course was later. After meeting Marie-Thérèse, Picasso, in a role straight out of *Commedia dell'Arte*, got around her mother, Émilie Marguerite. As an aging, benevolent, wealthy friend of the family, extremely devoted to this beautiful young girl, it became quite acceptable for the kind and famous artist to take

---

[12]   Lydia GASMAN, *Mystery, Magic and Love in Picasso, 1925-1938*, Ph.D Thesis, Columbia University, 1981, p.63,64,65.

[13]   John RICHARDSON, Preface-*Through the Eye of Picasso*, 1928-1934, "Picasso and Marie-Thérèse Walter", Beadleston Inc., Exhib. New York, 1985.

her along with his son Paulo, out to the circus, the movies, or the amusement parks. Predictably, little Paulo was soon left at home.

As for Marie-Thérèse, who conducted her love affair with aplomb and finesse, and who was not in the least intimidated by either her good-natured mother or her supportive sister, she would never have destroyed her early portraits as Richardson hypothesizes. The Marie-Thérèse I encountered in 1974 was fanatical about Picasso, and throughout her chequered life she had zealously hoarded even the tiniest scraps given to her by the artist[14].

So it does seem that it would have been out of character for either of them to have destroyed these "early portraits."

If that is the case, why were these early sketches destroyed? If Picasso and Marie-Thérèse had indeed not met until January 1927, then there is no dearth of "coded paintings" by Picasso, mostly in the form of musical instruments with allegorical symbolist objects and Marie-Thérèse's initials "M.T." at times combined with Picasso's "P" incorporated into them; there is even a nude figure of Marie-Thérèse in *The Painter's Studio* [15], a lithograph by Picasso in 1927 (Fig.16).

In 1971 and 1972 Marie-Thérèse gave a number of interviews to Lydia Gasman during which she talked of her life with Picasso. Extremely lonely, kind-hearted, emotionally still living in the past, and most certainly not meaning to cause harm, Marie-Thérèse described to Gasman some of the most intimate details of her life as Picasso's "Femme Enfant[16]". Only belatedly did she realize that if her disclosures became public knowledge, they might cause her personal problems, affect her married daughter, who was referred to in them, and cause

---

[14]   Marie-Thérèse, conversation with the author, 1974, Menton.

[15]   Georges BLOCH, *Pablo Picasso- Catalogue of the Printed Graphic Work 1904-1967*, Kornfeld & Klipstein, Berne, 1968.

[16]   Lydia GASMAN, *supra* note 12, p. 1422

great embarrassment to Picasso, who was still alive, and who frightened her terribly. "In his presence I trembled and kept my head bowed," she had told Gasman[17].

Gasman herself relates an incident in which Picasso, on receiving an innocuous poem by Marie-Thérèse's, reacted in his fury, by hiring a lawyer with every intention of suing her![18] And Marie-Thérèse was only too well aware of the furore caused by the publication of Françoise Gilot's book, *Life with Picasso* [19] which contained nothing comparable to some of the intimate details that Marie-Thérèse had revealed to Gasman.

That Marie-Thérèse afterwards became deeply disturbed on account of these disclosures, there can be no doubt. On the 20th of January 1972, she sent Gasman an imploring letter: "Les souvenirs de ma vie avec Pablo, il ne faut pas en parler, vous savez pourquoi."[20] In the years that followed, Marie-Thérèse's loneliness, withdrawal, and estrangement even from her daughter, increased.

Josep Palau i Fabre who prepared the Barcelona Exhibition Catalogue of 1977 "Picasso's Children Sketches," from Marie-Thérèse's collection, remarked "that she looked very strange and disturbed, and for a similar exhibition in Brussels, had insisted on having Picasso's love letters in the form of a heart prominently displayed"[21].

---

[17] Lydia GASMAN, *supra* note 12, p.1517

[18] Lydia GASMAN, *supra* note 12, p.1517

[19] *supra* note 8

[20] Lydia GASMAN, *supra* note 12, p. 1444

[21] Josep Palau i Fabre, conversations with the author, 1984, 1985, Barcelona.

Only a few days before her suicide in October 1977, Marie-Thérèse phoned Ines Sassier[22] "for Ines to visit her at once, concerning the most urgent and serious matter". But Ines, with a sick husband on her hands, could not make it...

In October 1977, subdued and looking strange, Marie-Thérèse talked briefly to a passing acquaintance who, in 1973, had viewed an exhibition of her Picasso collection in Geneva. This acquaintance casually asked Marie-Thérèse: "So you had known Monsieur Picasso for 50 years?" For a while Marie-Thérèse looked startled, and then she replied: "Fifty years? It was even longer than that." This acquaintance, whose identity I am not at liberty to disclose, years later told me about this meeting; bearing in mind that in 1977 Marie-Thérèse was freed of some of the restraints imposed on her by Picasso, her reply seems significant.[23]

Thus, the remarkable resemblance of the subject in *The Seated Girl*, 1926, to some of the early portraits and photos of Marie-Thérèse, the analyses by Brydon Smith and Vivian Barnett of *The Seated Girl* 1926, in relation to Picasso's *Seated Woman* of 1926-1927, the striking similarity of the "Sculptural Sketches," the earliest of which was dated 20 March 1926 to Picasso's Boisgeloup sculptures and paintings of Marie-Thérèse in the thirties, and the pertinent observation of Pierre Daix concerning "The Hidden Portrait of Marie-Thérèse" in *The Still Life with Musical Instruments*, *circa* 1925, all appeared to me to be more than coincidental.

---

22   Ines Sassier, conversations with the author, 1983, 84, 85, Mougins. To this day, Ines blames herself bitterly for not having seen Marie-Thérèse in October 1977. During the Second World War, Picasso got into the habit of taking his housekeeper Ines on his weekly visits to Marie-Thérèse and Maya. Ines became very friendly with Marie-Thérèse.

23   The crucial point of "X's" reference:
X: "You've known Monsieur Picasso for 50 years?" Marie-Thérèse: "Fifty years? It was even longer than that." She could have meant that she had met Picasso before January 1927, but, in October 1977, it was fifty years and several months since that first encounter if it had taken place in January 1927.

With these observations in mind, I felt that it would be logical to re-examine Picasso's oeuvre of 1926 in search of clues concerning Marie-Thérèse's statement of October 1977, shortly before her death: "Fifty years? It was even longer than that."

Was it possible for Picasso in these 1926 portraits to have prefigured Marie-Thérèse? And could one rely on Picasso's verbal statement to Françoise Gilot that his first meeting with Marie-Thérèse took place in January 1927? A contradictory and complex personality, Picasso was well known for flatly denying evidence when it did not suit him.[24] It was known that he had falsified the origin of his sketches in Zervos' Cahiers d'Arts (Z-VIII-283), by writing on them "Paris" instead of "Juan-les-Pins", or Boulogne (Fig.18). His evasions, falsifications, and secrecy as such do not concern us. But what made them necessary in the first place?

---

[24] Pierre CABANNE, *Pablo Picasso*, New York, William Morrow Co. Inc,, 1977, p. 368.

Picasso and the Surrealist Manifesto.

In the years preceding Picasso's encounter with Marie-Thérèse, there was no longer any doubt of his involvement with the Surrealist movement. The Surrealist Manifesto of André Breton[25], and similar views expressed by Aragon, Bataille, Desnos, Rimbaud, and later Éluard, proclaimed "l'amour fou" to be the pivotal part of one's visionary and creative existence and the search for eternal love, personified in the virginal purity and innocence of "la Femme Enfant."

Basically a sentimental cynic, well aware of human follies and inconsistencies, Picasso accepted the Surrealist credo because it personally suited him. But years later, he would rally against Éluard and blame the Surrealists for "the derangement of the senses", which caused the plight of Dora Maar, and then obscenely taunted Aragon for his continued love with Elsa! Meanwhile in the summer of 1926, accompanied by his wife Olga and little Paulo, Picasso was at Juan-les-Pins and champing at the bit, because Olga, that little ex-ballerina, turned out to be a veritable monster. A violent tyrannical woman, she made his life hell. Pretentious, with high society aspirations, she dragged him along the Riviera from one social function to another, and forced him to wear the formal, stylish clothes he once longed for, but now, fed up with conventions, detested.

A true bohemian, not bound to anyone, nourished in the rebellious ferment of Barcelona, Montmartre, and Montparnasse,

---

[25] André BRETON, *La Révolution Surréaliste*, 1924, No.1, p.24

disenchanted with his nagging wife, the glitter and absurdities of the roaring twenties on that ultra chic Côte d'Azur, Picasso could not have been more receptive to the Surrealist credo of "la Femme Enfant."

> "He returns once more to his autobiographic painting, his personal diary, henceforth his affective life, pains, joy, love, revolt which would express themselves directly."[26]

In this Summer of 1926 Picasso, at Juan-les-Pins "writes" his famous "Journal." Its pages are not numbered, and it is a veritable jumble of seemingly unrelated images, but within it dwells Picasso's alter ego, "The Bearded Painter," in a variety of disguises. He wears a Greek chlamys and chiton, and at times viny leaves crown his temple. Or, in short working pants, he sits in front of his easel and gravely contemplates his models, Olga in classical attire or Ukrainian embroidery, nudes, and figures of antiquity. Frequently he is burly, his bearded face bemused, sensitive, or stupid as he oscillates in this kaleidoscopic vista of unconnected images: Russian ballet dancers, harlequins, groups of soulful women, the Mediterranean sea. Soon, under his watchful gaze, a young woman undresses, then he watches her asleep: Olga, behaves most strangely and usurps his cane... while a young man is urgently expostulating with him on a weighty matter; a young girl unexpectedly appears, carrying a basket of flowers, while under his reproachful gaze a confrontation takes place between a burly, heavy set Sage, who seems to be pleading his case, and the oblivious Olga, still with his cane; the young girl appears once more; nude under her windblown robe, she pulls him toward her... No words are necessary to describe Picasso's conflict and drama on that sun-drenched shore at Juan-les-Pins.

---

26   Pierre CABANNE, *supra* note 24, p.242

The Bearded Painter's Saga
Juan-les-Pins 1926

"Picasso's Art is autobiographical through and through.
Indeed so close is the association between the subjects of his paintings and the man himself, that their evolution seems to run parallel with his own."

Michel Leiris, 1954

Fig.6   *The Seated Model*, sketch, Juan-les-Pins, 1926.

"The Bearded Painter," wearing <u>a classical Greek chlamys over a short chiton</u>[27], paints a woman in a typical Ukrainian dress with its embroidered flowing skirt, apron, bodice and high collar. This woman resembles Olga, also represented in Z-VII-42 and 50, J-l-P, and, significantly, in *Woman with two Harlequins*, Z-VII-43, J-l-P, a likely reference to Olga's ballerina past.

---

27   In "The Bearded Painter's Saga", this classical Greek attire seems to symbolize the fashionable clothing Picasso had to wear on the Riviera.

Fig.7   *The Dialogue*, sketch, Juan-les-Pins, 1926.
Fig.8   *Man and Woman*, sketch, Juan-les-Pins, 1926.

Note that by accident or design the seascapes forming the background for these two consecutive sketches seem to have merged with each other. In Fig.7, the Bearded Painter seems to be in transition; he is <u>no longer wearing his classic chlamys and chiton but has a towel wrapped around his middle</u>[28] and wears a crown of flowers. In his hand he holds a horseshoe, surely a sign of luck. His eyes seem puzzled; this alter ego of Picasso, who himself used to comb the beaches of Juan-les-Pins, is looking into the distance as if trying to guess his approaching fate. It does not take long to materialize in the form of a woman undressing. Fig.8: the Bearded Painter's transformation is now complete; <u>in shorts</u>[29], his chin supported on a cane, he watches the woman intently.

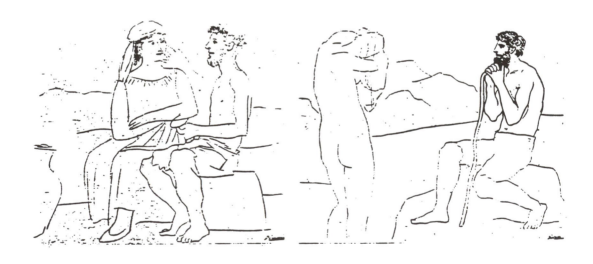

---

[28]   THE TOWEL here symbolizes a "state of change" or "in between state," in which the Bearded Painter decides what "clothing" he will wear or, to put in its historical perspective, whether to continue his restricted life with the fashionable Olga, or to choose the artistic freedom with this unknown nude.

[29]   SHORTS: symbol of artistic freedom and informality.

Fig.9   *Man and Sleeping Woman*, sketch, Juan-les-Pins, 1926.

A young woman sleeps under the Bearded Painter's watchful gaze. He is wearing <u>shorts</u> and supports his hand on a cane.

Fig.10 *Four Persons*, sketch, Juan-les-Pins, 1926.

"Confrontation": A heavy-set bearded Sage in a toga expostulates with a young woman who has usurped the Bearded Painter's cane[30]. She is wearing the classical attire of a Greek player or actress: ungirt chiton, and a veil over her head. This seems to be Olga; compare with *Olga in a Blue Veil* circa 1921, Fig.11. The heavy-set man seems to be pleading on behalf of the Bearded Painter, who again is wearing his classical chlamys over the short chiton. Trustingly he puts his hand on the shoulder of the heavy-set bearded Sage, while the likeness of Olga supports herself on the shoulder of a performer in Ukrainian, or Bessarabian bulbous pants, collarless shirt, and narrow waistcoat, Picasso's pointed reference to her ballerina past.

---

30 CANE: in "The Bearded Painter's Saga", Picasso uses it as a symbol of self reliance and authority.

Fig.11 *The Blue Veil,* oil on canvas, 1921.

Olga wearing the ungirt chiton and a veil over her head in the classical attire of a Greek player or actress.

Fig.12 *Three Persons*, sketch, Juan-les-Pins, 1926.

Two women confront each other. The woman resembling Olga, in a long chiton, with a veil over her head, and pointedly holding up the Bearded Painter's cane, confronts a younger girl, wearing a flowing robe, a long shawl around her head, and possibly a flower wreath. In her hand the girl: holds a basket of flowers. From behind, looking surreptitiously on this scene, the Bearded Painter is holding a flower[31] in his hand. No longer in shorts or chiton, he has a towel wrapped around his middle.

---

31   FLOWER: the symbol of love.

Fig.13 *The Discourse*, sketch, Juan-les-Pins, 1926.

The Bearded Painter, wearing <u>shorts</u> again, supports himself on his cane and gravely listens to an impassionate discourse by a young man who looks remarkably like André Breton, while another young listener (could it be Desnos?)[32] sits beside him.

---

[32] Picasso identified himself with Breton, whose novel *Nadja* was based on his chance encounter with Nadja at the Place de l'Opéra in Paris, and thus recalled Picasso's own "miraculous" meeting with Marie-Thérèse. Robert Desnos, one of the most gifted of the surrealist writers, was a frequent visitor to the Riviera.

Fig.14 *Three Persons*, sketch, 1926.

"Parting Scene": <u>The Bearded Painter in shorts, with his cane restored,</u> stands between the two women. He has obviously decided what course to follow; his cane (authority) and shorts (freedom) indicate it clearly. Remorseful, he extends his left hand to the woman resembling Olga, as if he was leaving her. The Bearded Painter can no longer avoid his fate in the form of a voluptuous young hoyden, naked under a wind-blown robe, curvaceous, firm breasted, heavy and fleshy of leg. The girl puts her arm around the Bearded Painter's neck, and envelops him in her flowing robe, Z-VII-17; 1926, Paris. The Bearded Painter's desire is overpowering, and his shorts can barely conceal it. It is significant that this sketch unlike the others, is not marked Juan-les-Pins but Paris. Compare the woman on the right of this sketch with Olga in 1926 (Fig.15).

And thus ends Picasso's "Bearded Painter's Saga" for 1926.

Fig.15 *Woman's Profile*, sketch, Juan-les-Pins, 1926.

Olga in classical Greek attire.

Fig.16 *The Painter's Studio*, eau-forte, 1927.

The following year 1927 in Paris, brings *The Painter's Studio* for Balzac's, *Le chef d'oeuvre inconnu*.

The same Bearded Painter, in shorts, works busily on a canvas. At his side, watching him, and leaning over Picasso's old armchair, is a beautiful young nude; she is undoubtedly Marie-Thérèse[33]. Compare the profile of the nude model's face in the sketch with that of Marie-Thérèse in a photo, *circa* 1927 (Photo 2).

The Bearded Painter making love to his beautiful model[34], 1927, not illustrated here, marks the progression of Picasso's love affair with Marie-Thérèse.

---

33   BLOCH, *supra* note 15 p.43, Pl.89.

34   BLOCH, *supra* note 15 p.39, Pl.77.

Photo 2 Marie-Thérèse Walter, circa 1927.
          Collection Maya Ruiz Picasso.

The Juan-les-Pins sketch-book of 1926, recorded in Zervos Volume No.7., contains altogether twenty-two sketches, many of which, however, are repetitive, as, for example,

"The Bearded Painter at work":   Z-VII-37,44,45 and 47;
"Olga in company of women":   Z-VII-42,53;
"Portraits of Olga":   Z-VII-34,35,36,50.

Nevertheless, there is no doubt that, even taken alone, the fourteen sketches described by me in "The Bearded Painter's Saga", provide ground for conjecture. It is possible that related sketches, not recorded in Zervos, exist, and that they will make it necessary to revise in depth my interpretation of "The Bearded Painter's Saga". But in their absence, the evidence presented here is eloquent. The numerous portraits of Olga, dispersed through the pages of Picasso's "Journal," fit in well with the painter's desire for secrecy.

Thus, it seemed remarkable not only that Picasso in early 1926, had prefigured Marie-Thérèse in the "col Claudine" and striped dress which he would portray in subsequent years, but also, that, in the summer of 1926, he had reflected in his Juan-les-Pins Journal his difficulties with Olga, his adoption of the Surrealist credo of "l'amour fou," and his discovery of "la Femme-Enfant." In the remarkable "Parting Scene" (Fig.14), Picasso seems to portray the future. What is more likely, is that an autobiographical event is already in progress as accompanied by the nude young girl, the Bearded Painter leaves the older woman. And in this saga Picasso leaves no doubt as to the identity of the older woman, indicated in a number of pointed references to her Russian ancestry and her association with the dancers and performers of Les Ballets Russes.

The autobiographical nature of "The Bearded Painter's Saga" can no longer be disregarded as a mere conjecture, since the saga itself is linked logically to Picasso's own documented, historical events that were soon to follow.

But "The Bearded Painter's Saga" poses some puzzling questions if we accept the hypothesis that the Bearded Painter's heroine is Marie-Thérèse. Had Picasso secreted her at Juan-les-Pins as early as 1926? He would do that two years later, when he placed her in a pension for children at Dinard. And in 1930, she was with him at Juan-les-Pins. Is it possible that Picasso met her before 1926, and carried her romantic image onto the pages of his Juan-les-Pins Journal?

Alone "The Bearded Painter's Saga" of 1926, does not offer a satisfactory explanation of Picasso's early relationship with Marie-Thérèse. It is significant however, that, unlike the others, "The Parting Scene" (Fig.14), in which the "Bearded Painter" took leave of the older woman, is placed not in Juan-les-Pins but in Paris.

Picasso's secrecy over his relationship with Marie-Thérèse.

The Saga of the Bearded Painter's "amour fou" for his "Femme Enfant" continues for a number of years after Picasso's acknowledged encounter with Marie-Thérèse in January 1927. Marie-Thérèse is undoubtedly his greatest love. The Bearded Painter paints, sculpts, and plays his flute (Fig.17), and under her spell he reaches sublime heights of poetry, while through the passion of "l'amour fou", violent and on heat, he unleashes a torrent of surrealist and erotic images. However, his need for secrecy is so great, that even after twenty years of intimacy during which he created thousands of sketches, prints, paintings, and sculptures of her, Marie-Thérèse is not once mentioned in the voluminous catalogues of his faithful recorder, Zervos!

This secrecy is also reflected in the general titles given to the sketches and paintings of Marie-Thérèse's mother and sisters: *Woman, Young Girl, Head of a Girl, Woman with Spectacles* etc. After the birth of his and Marie-Thérèse's daughter Maya in 1935, Picasso's tender paintings of her and Marie-Thérèse are described in Zervos as simply *Mother and Child*. Not until 1939 is this child's name noted in Zervos as "Maya," but the mother holding her apparently has no name! Marie-Thérèse is never named; yet as soon as Picasso became acquainted with Dora Maar, he named her prominently in his work! Was this the superstitious Picasso hoping not to offend the omnipotent gods with his hubris in taking possession of a very young girl? Hoping to keep the evil spirits away from his joy and happiness by not mentioning her name, but only her initials

Fig.17 *Reclining Nude and Flute Player*, Boisgeloup, oil and china ink, September 1932.

Observe the Bearded Painter's profile on the nude's face.

"M.T"? Hoping to hide her even from his destructive *alter ego*, the blind and hypochondriac Minotaur?

Ever adhering to his code of utmost secrecy, Picasso titles his sketches obscurely and falsifies their location. For example in *The Artist's Son*, a work Picasso claimed to have painted in Paris on 13 October 1935, Paulo, his son, is actually Picasso himself, reading before a shadowy outline of Marie-Thérèse tending their newborn baby. That day, Picasso had in fact been in Boulogne visiting Marie-Thérèse at the medical clinic where she had given birth[35], (Fig.18).

Picasso is only too well aware of the dark, destructive forces that his psyche could produce, and he tries to keep them at bay by representing scenes of great tenderness and beauty, such as *Mother and Child* (Z-VII-346, February 1937, and Z-IX-230 and 231, 1938) in which he portrays Marie-Thérèse with the infant baby or in his lovely sketches and paintings of their daughter Maya, whom he adores (Z-IX-229, November 1938).

But once Marie-Thérèse has grown up, she is no longer the forbidden fruit; now he can taste her freely. She ceases to be the "Femme-Enfant" of his surrealistic dreams, and suddenly the whole tension and drama of their relationship disappears; no more mystery, no breathless encounters, no surreptitious sex. Moreover, after the experience of his domestic unhappiness with Olga, Picasso is deadly

---

[35] Marie-Thérèse gave birth to "Maya" (Maria de la Conception) on 6 October 1935 in Boulogne's Belvedère Medical Clinic, which Picasso visited on Sunday, 13 October 1935. The likeness in this sketch is undoubtedly of a "glamourized" Picasso, rather than of his son Paulo, while in the background Marie-Thérèse is tending the baby. Compare this sketch of "Paulo" Fig. 18 to a photo of Picasso in 1935(Photo 3). Picasso, accompanied by Marie-Thérèse's sister, went to register the birth of his child with the notation: "Father unknown". Years later, when Marie-Thérèse had their daughter baptized, Picasso is described on the certificate as: "Godfather."
All paintings and sketches fully dated by Picasso as to year, month, and day had for him a special significance.

Fig.18 *The Artist's Son*, china ink, "Paris", Sunday 13 October
1935.
(Compare with Photo 3.)

Photo 3 Picasso, Paris, 1935.
     G. Brassai

afraid of another domestic entanglement and shows his feelings clearly! (Fig.19) He feels himself trapped by his young mistress, and to punish her, he hides behind the beastly mask of the Minotaur. Sadistic, violent, and bent on rape, he destroys her image. The reason for this destruction is obvious, after creating thousands of images of her, Picasso has exhausted his artistic vocabulary for Marie-Thérèse.

Meanwhile, as a sense of impending doom hangs over Europe, the Bearded Painter, confused and afraid, begins to search for a different muse, and finds her in the brilliant, weeping Dora Maar, who will accompany him through a long period of darkness and tragedy. In an autobiographical statement, he sits enthroned, one hand supported on a cane, and majestically waits while at a partly opened door, Dora Maar, hesitating, as if she knew that once in she could not retreat, enters his life (Z-VIII-295, 1 August 1936).

A long period of sadness and isolation begins for Marie-Thérèse at Tremblay-sur-Mauldre, Vollard's country estate. Picasso visits her there from time to time, and he commemorates the second birthday of their daughter, 6 October 1937, in a typical Picassian sketch (Fig.20). He also portrays Marie-Thérèse as blind, with fish (scales) over her eyes (Fig.21), but just the same, keeps on sending her letters full of love...

In years to come, Picasso's *alter ego* "The Bearded Painter" will emerge frequently in the artist's oeuvre. "The Bearded Painter" paints, sculpts, and makes love, but his passion, tenderness, and violence lack the dramatic quality they had had in his earlier days. In time he becomes pot-bellied, short-sighted and vacuous; is surrounded by luscious nudes he is unable to seduce; becomes a sad reflexion on the pathos of advancing age. But, undaunted, he continues to paint, and he weaves his dramatic past into a winter of illusions.

This historical digression was necessary in order to place *The Seated Girl*, done by Picasso in 1926 (Fig.4), a) in its chronological perspective vis-à-vis "The Bearded Painter's Saga", b) in perspective of Picasso's extreme secrecy about his liaison with Marie-Thérèse, and

Fig.19 *Birds in a Cage*, oil on canvas, 1937.

Fig.20   *Standing Woman* (!), pencil sketch, Paris, 6 October 1937.

Fig.21   *Woman's Head with Fish*, pencil sketch, 1937.

finally, c) in historical presentation of Picasso—Marie-Thérèse relationship vis-à-vis Picasso's "double images".

Picasso's "double images."

I will now comment more fully on the aspect of secrecy in Picasso's relationship with Marie-Thérèse, which is reflected in his paintings, and more particularly on the significance of his "double images" of 1926 (Fig.5 b,c and d) one of which was noted in *The Seated Girl* (Fig.4). The "double image" in Fig.4 is similar to the ones described in Fig.5; contained within the left side of the girl's face is the dark profile of a man's face and neck, its base, formed by the Peter Pan collar, being an integral part of the composition. Later, I shall analyze the occurrence of this technique in Picasso's oeuvre from 1920 until 1939.

For the moment, however, let us observe carefully the startled, if not shocked, expression of the girl. What is disturbing her so much? Most likely the answer lies in the book or sketch-book that she holds open in her lap. According to Gasman, Picasso introduced Marie-Thérèse to sex by having her admire the erotic water colours of Isidro Nonell and pictures of young girls in the company of older men[36]. If our suppositions are correct, *The Seated Girl* of 1926 would date to the early period of Picasso's intimate relationship with Marie-Thérèse. Note that the girl is sitting in Picasso's old armchair, the one relegated by Olga to his studio upstairs, where she never visited, but where Marie-Thérèse went frequently.

Closely related to *The Seated Girl* is *Standing Girl*, also done in 1926 (Fig.22). In this sketch, the figure is more stylized. The girl is

[36]   Lydia GASMAN, *supra* note 12

53

Fig 22   *Standing Girl*, pen and ink, 1926.

wearing a striped dress; the left breast pushes it out. On her head, a bell shaped fringed hat. She is standing in what appears to be a doorway, and it is raining outside. Behind her there is a dark figure with prominent left leg, buttock, and back, its arm and hand resting over the girl's hand and arm. The dark figure extends upwards and dissects the frontal aspect of the girl's face with four heavy vertical stripes, those on the left side forming a distinct profile which looks to the right. Thus, the dark figure in the back merges with, and encompasses, the standing girl through a combination of frontal and lateral configurations.

In *The Seated Woman* of 1926-1927 (Fig.23), Picasso pushed the stylization and abstraction of *The Seated Girl* (Fig.4) much further. As early as 1967 Brydon Smith noted that the pen and ink sketch, *Seated Girl*, "seemed to be the basis of the painting[37] *The Seated Woman*, Art Gallery of Ontario Collection, and furthermore, the latter had great personal significance for Picasso, and which he changed considerably, and worked on for a long time, before being satisfied that it was complete." *The Seated Woman*, dated on the back 1926-1927, is of tremendous significance for my study, not only because of its relation to *The Seated Girl*, 1926, but also because of Picasso's acknowledgment that he knew Marie-Thérèse since early January 1927. To quote Brydon Smith again: "Like in the sketch and the painting, the woman [assumed to be Olga] is wearing a striped dress with horizontally striped neckline [col Claudine]. She sits with her arms crossed over an open book on her lap..." And Brydon continues: "The most disquieting aspect of this painting is the head, which is the combination of three heads in one: the large flat profile on the left has strongly marked features of eye, forehead, nose mouth and chin which seems to be masculine in form. <u>The long round profile of the back of the head resembles Picasso's own head shape, as seen in profile photographs and also certain self portraits.</u> The child like profile on the back has a high

---

[37]   Brydon SMITH, *supra* note 9.

Fig.23   *Seated Woman,* 1926-27.

forehead and weaker features and looks up to the larger profile with apparent bewilderment and apprehension..."

Twenty years ago, when Brydon Smith was making these astute observations, the details of Picasso's intimate life with Marie-Thérèse were a closely guarded secret. Today, armed with hindsight, we can look at the relationship with a different eye and hypothesize a progression of the intimacy between Picasso and the young Marie-Thérèse. This hypothesis would be supported by the date of that painting 1926-1927. It has been suggested to me that the book the *Seated Woman* is holding might be by the Marquis de Sade, much favoured by Picasso when introducing his partners to sex[38]. As in *The Seated Girl* (Fig.4), the subject in *Seated Woman* (Fig.23) is bewildered and uneasy. But she has lost some of the static quality present in the subject of the sketch. There is movement here, and violence; hair falls to one side, the widely open mouth exclaims in shocked surprise; the right breast is fully exposed as she is drawn to Picasso, and locked in by his all encompassing likeness in a gesture of erotic foreplay, or in frank assault. The erotic component of their relationship was illustrated again by Picasso in *Étreinte*, 1927 in which Marie-Thérèse's features are discernible (Bloch 39, ill.77). The meaning of the second silhouette in the painting as described by Smith is not quite clear. That silhouette may represent the turning of the face or more likely, Picasso's all embracing presence.

There can be no doubt that Picasso's "double images" expressed his complete identification with, and possession of, Marie-Thérèse. But there is another meaning to these "double images" which Picasso so skillfully executed: his jealousy! Picasso was swept off his feet by Marie-Thérèse. Her youth, radiance, and fairness, and the sensual, nonchalant way in which she carried herself obsessed him. In addition, once Picasso had aroused Marie-Thérèse's dormant sexuality his fears and insecurity increased. He was terrified that she might

---

[38]   Conversations with Geneviève Laporte, Paris, 1985-86.

leave him for a younger man, and he often accused her of infidelity. To ensure his possession of her, and to ward off "evil influences," the superstitious Picasso transformed her through his images of himself, undoubtedly shadowy *alter egos*, jealous and possessive guardian spirits of Marie-Thérèse. He watched over her constantly, and surrounded her with images of his watchfulness, his portraits hanging over her, his silhouette in the doorway, his face in the window, like a peeping Tom, and even the statues by the Bearded Sculptor, which fix her in a steady gaze. For a number of years these "double images," breathing the presence of Picasso, were practically inseparable from portraits and sketches of Marie-Thérèse.

Picasso had used "double images" in the past, but they had consisted only of <u>frontal and lateral projections of the same face</u>. Thus the "double image" incorporating Picasso's own representation was new to his *oeuvre*, and because of its obvious reference to Marie-Thérèse, I subjected it to careful scrutiny.

I compared the occurrence of "double images" during the acknowledged period of Marie-Thérèse's presence, starting in 1927, with their occurrence in the years 1920-1927. The findings are presented in Graph 1.

This analysis was subject to the limitation that not all of Picasso's production was available to me. Nonetheless, after perusing 1104 works and excluding all controversial material, I was left with 170 "double images." However, this figure had to be revised dramatically following publication of Picasso's sketch-books in November 1986, towards the end of my study [39].

These sketch-books provided me with a rich source of material for the extension of this work, and in the end I had no fewer than 301 such representations. While reviewing my data, it soon became

---

39   Arnold and Marc GLIMCHER (ed.), *Je Suis le Cahier*, London, Thames and Hudson Ltd., 1986.

evident that Picasso's "double images" consisted of four distinctives types: a) face- "double-image"; b) full body- "double-image"; c) mixed type, which included Picasso's "double-image" and Picasso's "outside" representation; d) Picasso's "outside" representations only. The "outside" representations of Picasso were not included in this study, since the information I was looking for, emerged from the study of the first three types. Furthermore, the general pattern of Picasso's "outside" representations, closely approximated the one found in the first three types.

Illustrations of Picasso's "double-images"

Face "double-image":   Figs.4; 5b- c- d; 17; 24; 25;
                                        26; 27; 28; 29; 30; 31; 32; 33.

Full body "double-image":   Figs. 22; 23; 34; 35; 55.

Mixed "double-image" and Picasso's "outside" representation:
                                        Figs. 36; 50.

Picasso's "outside" representation only: Figs. 37; 38; 39; 40.

The years 1920 to 1924 served as a baseline; no "double images" were found. And then, in February 1925 appeared the first "double image" (Fig.24). It was followed by another two in July. From then until December, their incidence increased dramatically — there were no fewer than 37 of which a large number could be related to *L'Atelier de la Modiste* of January 1926 (Fig.50). Production of "double images" continued without interruption in 1926 and was centered on portraits of an "unknown young woman" such as *The Seated Girl* (Fig.4), and the *Sculptural Sketches* (Fig.5). That year alone, there were no fewer than 64 such representations!

However, the most important aspect of this production was that it continued uninterruptedly at a high level in following years. This discovery was of tremendous significance, since from January 1927 we were into the "generally acknowledged" period of the Picasso/Marie-Thérèse relationship. Graph 1

Fig.24   *Woman's Head*, oil on canvas, 1924-25.

Fig.25   *Woman's Head*, lithograph, November 1925.

Fig.26   Sketch, Paris, March 1926.

Fig.27   Sketch, Paris, March 1926.

Fig.28   Sketch, Paris, March 1926.

Fig.29　Sketch, Paris, March 1926.

Fig.30 *Head of a Young Girl,* oil on canvas, November 1926.

Fig.31　*Head*, oil on board, 22 November 1929.

Fig.32   *Woman's Head*, oil on canvas, 1929.

Fig.33 Sketch, china ink, Paris, 15 January 1934.

Fig.34 *Seated Girl*, July 1925.

Fig.35　Sketch, Paris, March 1926.

Fig.36 *The Sculptor*, oil on canvas, Paris, 7 December 1931.

Fig.37 *Figure and Profile,* oil on canvas, 1927-28.

Fig.38　*Painter and Model,* oil on canvas, Paris, 1928.

Fig.39   *Seated Nude*, eau-forte, July 1931.

Fig.40 *Woman Holding a Book*, oil on canvas, 1932.

Table for Graph 1

```
1920 ------------------0
1921 ------------------0
1922 ------------------0
1923 ------------------0
1924 ------------------0
1925 ---------------- 40
1926 ---------------- 64
1927 ---------------- 35
1928 ---------------- 30
1929 ---------------- 25
1930 ---------------- 28
1931 ---------------- 42
1932 ----------------- 6
1933 ----------------- 6
1934 ----------------- 5
1935 ----------------- 8
1936 ----------------- 8
1937 ----------------- 3
1938 ----------------- 1
1939 ----------------- 0
1940 ----------------- 0
```

Since the analysis of the "double images" provided me with important clues for a large part of this study, let us examine two in particular, one done in February 1925 (Fig.24) and the other done in November (Fig.25).

Graph 1

Picasso's "double images" for the years 1920 to 1926,
preceding the generally "accepted period" of
Marie-Thérèse Walter (8 January 1927), and
afterwards.
The "outside representations" of Picasso are not
included in this graph.

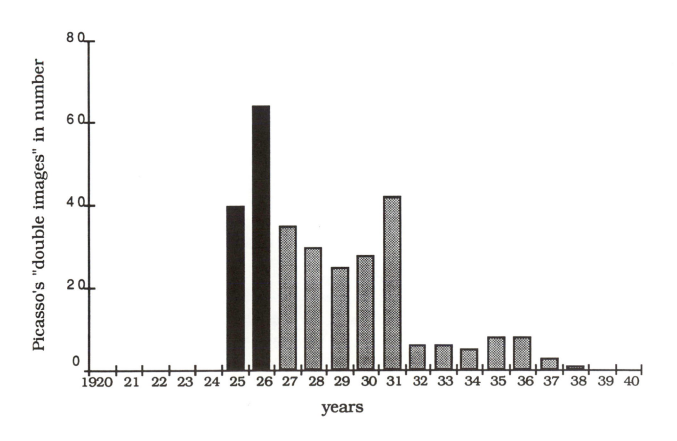

The Woman's Head [40] (Fig.24), face-"double-image", oil portrait on canvas, started by Picasso in 1924 and completed in February 1925, shows a young woman with winged hair, the long nose almost bisecting her face, the chin and left side of which are resting in the palm of the left hand. That hand also supports the left side of the "double image," which is formed by contrasting the grey right half of the face with the whitish grey left half. The division is further enhanced by the nose, which turns on the forehead at a right angle in place of an eyebrow, thus giving the appearance of an angular profile on the left of the face, looking to its right. The observer senses, strangely, grave introspection on the girl's face and tension between the opposing halves, effects masterfully obtained by Picasso with only a few lines. Compare this painting to an almost identical image in the sculptural sketch (20 March 1926, Fig.5 c).

The lithograph *Woman's Head* of November 1925[41], (Fig.25), face "double-image" of a young fair-haired girl, "prefigures" Marie-Thérèse in early photos and pencil sketches in the Maya Ruiz Picasso collection, and bears a striking resemblance to the representation of the young girl in *The Parting Scene* of "The Bearded Painter's Saga" of 1926 (Fig.14). This important lithograph will be discussed later in connection with Picasso's dry-point sketches and other related work of November 1925.

Not only do the "double images" representing these "unknown young women", who strongly resemble Marie-Thérèse, demonstrate continuity with the "accepted" portraits of Marie-Thérèse, but beginning in 1926 one of the images starts to migrate outwards; the clear likeness of Picasso views these "young women" from outside, as in *L'Atelier de la Modiste*, January 1926 (Fig.50), and in *The Seated*

---

[40]　At the back of the canvas, in Picasso's handwriting: "Started 1924, finished February 1925".

[41]　BLOCH, *supra* note 15 p.39, Pl.73

Nude, July 1931 (Fig.39) In a number of instances the face of Picasso appears quite angry (Figs.31 and 32) while that of the "young woman" looks bewildered and uneasy (Figs. 4, 5c, 23, 24, 28 and 29) and even at times absolutely terrified (Figs.29 and 32). Assuming that these are representations of Marie-Thérèse, they confirm my observations[42] that Marie-Thérèse's secret affair with Picasso was far from easy, and that at times it put her under considerable strain.

To a remarkable extent Picasso's "double images" and "shadowy outside presences" parallel the course of his infatuation with Marie-Thérèse. Thus starting in 1939, when he had managed to instill in her feelings of submission and dependency, his ghosts were exorcised, and he ceased to create "double images" and veiled representations.

Certain results of this study of Picasso's "double images" were totally unexpected. I had strong and valid reasons to believe that Picasso's had met Marie-Thérèse before January 1927, based on the remarkable likeness of her in numerous portraits and sketches of 1926, and on Picasso's autobiographical statement in "The Bearded Painter's Saga" of that year. This supposition was merely confirmed by the findings on the "double images" of 1926 which demonstrated continuity into the "accepted" period of Marie-Thérèse's presence. However, the unexpected discovery of a "double image", in February 1925, when Marie-Thérèse was barely fifteen, followed by 39 more that same year raised a number of questions that I was unable to answer. It became clear that a study had to be made of all available Picassos from 1925 to 1940 in order to clarify the significance of the portraits and sketches of 1925, whose subject strikingly resembled Marie-Thérèse, and also to examine the possibility of their close relationship to certain of Picasso's major works, such as *La Statuaire*, July 1925 (Fig.55) and more importantly, *L'Atelier de la Modiste* of January 1926 (Fig.50).

Studying some of these Picassos was like learning a new pictorial language! His clandestine relationship with Marie-Thérèse was

---

[42] Author's interviews in France, October 1986

expressed in many different ways, as for example in his "comical cartoons," three of which are presented here, in which the message is obvious: "Sex on the 27 of March" and "Screaming Woman 28th" (Fig.41), the latter is reminiscent of Olga in *Nude in an Armchair* (Fig.2). The illustration Fig.42 is a sort of Picassian Decameron.

Fig.41   Sketch, china ink, 1928.

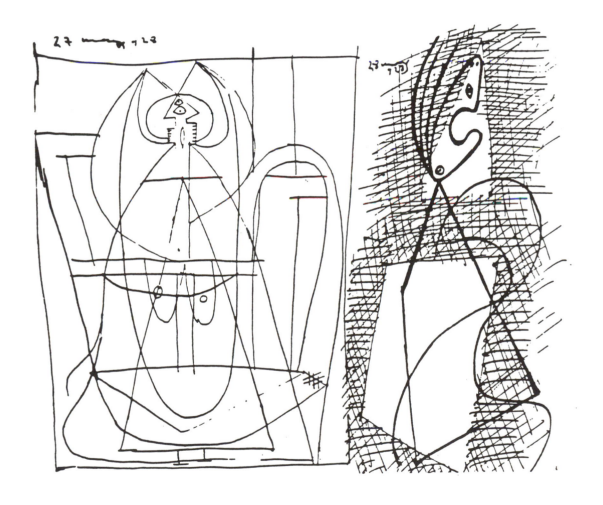

Fig.42   Sketch, pencil, 1928.

*Pierre Daix's Study of the hidden portrait
of Marie-Thérèse.*

One of the most important pictorial aspects of the secret relationship between Picasso and Marie-Thérèse is Picasso's codification in the *Musical Instruments*, mentioned earlier in this paper, of Marie-Thérèse's initials, "M.T," and, occasionally, his own "P." We will review this aspect further, but first we must consider a *Musical Instrument* in which Picasso's "code" for Marie-Thérèse was altogether different. And this leads me to Pierre Daix's study of *The Still Life with Musical Instruments* and *Reclining Dancer with Tambourine*[43] (Z-V-416, 1925).

After a thorough study of this painting, Daix concluded that the "Reclining Dancer" was in fact "the nude and recumbent Marie-Thérèse." And it would be difficult for anyone who looked at the work not to agree. However, there was a problem immediately noted by Daix, with the date of the painting: the work preceded by almost two years Picasso's meeting with Marie-Thérèse!

The *Still Life* was neither dated or signed, so the date recorded by Zervos must have come either directly from Picasso or indirectly through Picasso's secretary Sabartès. In order to reconcile this discrepancy in dates, Daix compared the *Still Life* (Z-V-416, 1925) with the similar *Non Figurative Still Life with Musical Instruments* (Z-VII-3, 1926) and concluded that "the *Still Life with Musical Instruments*

---

[43]   Pierre DAIX, *supra* note 11

circa 1925 was probably done by Picasso in 1926, and it stayed in his Studio long enough for Picasso to have inserted Marie-Thérèse in the painting soon after their meeting in 1927".

For me, this statement posed a number of problems. To begin with the title of the painting, which Zervos must have obtained from Picasso, was misleading since there was no tambourine and the girl depicted was not a dancer but Marie-Thérèse. Also since the very similar *Non Figurative Still Life* (Z-VII-3) is at the very beginning of the catalogue of works done in 1926, whereas the *Still Life with Musical Instruments* (Z-V-416) is found towards the end of the catalogue of works of 1925 , Daix's observations on the chronological closeness and stylistic similarity of the two still lifes seem to be perfectly confirmed. On the other hand, the relative positions of the works in the catalogues do not invalidate Zervos' dating of the *Still Life with Musical Instruments* and the nude Marie-Thérèse to late 1925. Finally, what would be the point in 1927 of Picasso's "hiding" her in a painting of 1925 when we know that in 1927 Picasso was making sketches of Marie-Thérèse, in which she is clearly represented, as for example the sitting nude in *The Painter's Studio* (Fig.16).

In 1925, however, Picasso had valid reasons for hiding Marie-Thérèse, his wife Olga for one. More importantly, in 1925 Marie-Thérèse was only 15.

Picasso in fact took great care that Marie-Thérèse was never seen bodily, even when he had her right under Olga's nose in Paris, Dinard, or Juan-les-Pins. He confided her presence only to his canvas, and with an artist as versatile as was Picasso, allusions to his secret life could take many forms.

Picasso's "Coded Musical Instruments".

Long before the advent of Marie-Thérèse in his life, Picasso was fond of portraying Musical Instruments, traditionally to begin with, and later, during his cubist period, geometrically and fragmented . In the early twenties these instruments assumed freer, more flowing forms, amoeboid articulated shapes, like pieces fitted in a jigsaw puzzle. This was Picasso's "curvilinear cubism". In the period 1924-1926, these free-flowing forms merged with the more geometrical and linear representations; the line became solid or broken within a round space or rectangle to form the style found in his "coded musical instruments".

After meeting Marie-Thérèse, Picasso inserted the initials M.T. and P. in the "Musical Instruments", thus "coding" them as a secret reference to the girl. Early in their relationship Picasso gave one of these "coded musical instruments" to Marie-Thérèse; it was not signed, dated, or recorded in Zervos. In the picture, projected through the strings of a guitar, is Picasso's own white hand, and over it the initials M.T. (Maya Ruiz Picasso coll.). The work is informally dated to 1927, but Daix himself notes that "this guitar appears to be a stylization of the large *Guitar* Z-V-6, made out of sackcloth [which] dates to the Spring of 1926." He explains the discrepancy in dates by hypothesizing "that Picasso in greeting Marie-Thérèse already had in mind forms dating from the previous year"[44]...

---

44   Pierre DAIX, *supra* note 11

Let us now consider Picasso's "coded musical instruments" illustrated in Zervos Z-VII-54,55,56 and 110. The first three are reproduced here in Figs.43. None of these works was signed or dated, but following information received from Picasso, Zervos inserted them in the 1927 section of the catalogue.

From a perusal of Zervos's catalogue of works done in 1926, it would appear that after finishing his Juan-les-Pins Carnet in September of that year, and returning from his holidays in Spain in October, Picasso executed only four oil paintings: the "double images" portraits of young girls one of which is dated November 1926.

Zervos' catalogue dates the "coded musical instruments" to 1927 immediately after the 1926 portraits. The strangeness of this dating was not lost on Zervos, but in 1932 when he started his massive catalogues, his task, however, was far from easy; by then Picassos were scattered all over the world, and to make matters worse Picasso was not always forthcoming. In fact, Picasso hid many of his works, keeping them strictly for himself. In 1956, when David Douglas Duncan asked Picasso how many works were hidden, the answer was: "about 3000"![45] Moreover, Picasso, whose visual memory was phenomenal, had great difficulty remembering dates; and to complicate matters further for the dedicated Zervos, he was not beyond improvisation, particularly if a work touched upon some intimate aspect of his life, one that he wished still to keep secret.

These observations are in no way intended to diminish the value of Zervos's monumental work; without it this study would have been impossible. They merely underline the fact that some at least of the undated illustrations in Zervos require a re-evaluation for dating based on a thorough comparative analysis, and, at times, on a

---

[45] David DOUGLAS DUNCAN, Conversation with Picasso, "La Californie", Cannes, 1956

Fig.43 "Coded musical instruments", oil on canvases, Paris, 1927.

Guitar on a Wall, oil on canvas, Paris 1927.

Guitar, oil on canvas, 1927.

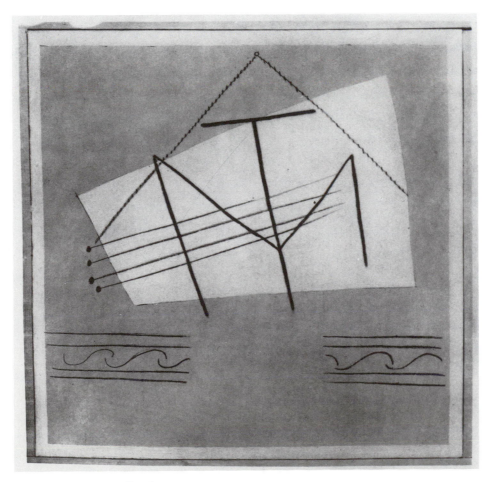

Guitar, oil on canvas, 1927.

detailed knowledge of Picasso's location and movements.

In 1955, as Volume 7 was going into press, Zervos and his collaborators found additional material which was added in the form of a supplement. It did nothing to account for a curious lack of Picassos in November and December 1926, but among the items included in it was another "coded" musical instrument containing, unmistakably, Marie-Thérèse's initials. This work, however, was different from the others we had studied to that point; it was signed and dated by Picasso, and the date on it was November 1925! (Fig.44). Where Zervos had hold of it, I do not know, and why he would have included it in his catalogue for 1926-1932 is a mystery. Before each publication of the *Cahiers d'Arts*, Zervos discussed all doubtful datings and controversial material with Picasso, but in this case, it must have seemed obvious that no controversy was possible since the work was signed and dated by Picasso. So Zervos inserted it in his supplement. Besides, Picasso was with Jacqueline in Vallauris; it has been suggested to me that the final proofs of Volume 7 were approved by Picasso's secretary, Sabartes[46].

In her voluminous dissertation, Gasman argues that this *Musical Instrument*, signed and dated with the initials "M.T."(Fig.44) was a tribute to Picasso's friend Guillaume Apollinaire, who died on the 9th of November 1918[47]. She suggests, following Leiris's analysis of magic letters, that "the distended M" represents in fact a spacious letter A," while the letter "T," enclosed within a circle, "is Tau cross," recalling Max Jacob's comments in "Saint Matorel" on Christ's mystical cross in the form of "T".[48]

---

[46] Conversation with Ines Sassier, Mougins, 1983-84-85-86.

[47] Lydia GASMAN, *supra* note 12, p.63, 64 and 65.

[48] Lydia GASMAN, *supra* note 12, p.951, Illustr. 264.

Fig.44 "Coded" *Musical Instrument*, china ink, November 1925.

In fact Gasman assumes that the other two *Musical Instruments* done in 1925 are also tribute to Apollinaire. In *Musical Instrument* (Pl. 1265 Gasman no.22 Fig.45), the letter "i", for example, refers to Guillaume Apollinaire and to his *Calligrammes*, which was republished in 1925. In *Musical Instrument* (Pl. 1266 Gasman no.22 Fig.46), the stylized "L" denotes the accented "L" in Guillaume Apollinaire, as well as, following Breton's and Leiris's interpretation of "L," the Hebrew "EL". The letter "K" represents Apollinaire's mother's maiden name, Kostrowitzky[49]...

It does not lie within scope of this work to analyse Gasman's extensive research into the kabbalistic, surrealistic, and automatist influences on Picasso's *Musical Instruments*. Gasman's reference to Theodore Reff's description of *The Three Musicians* 1921 as "Picasso's tribute to his best friends and bohemian youth, to the dead Apollinaire and estranged Max Jacob", does not support her arguments that Picasso's *Musical Instruments* of 1925 "are a modest tribute to Apollinaire".[50] Had the coded "M.T." in the *Musical Instrument* of 1925 been a tribute to Apollinaire, it is almost certain that it would have been dated 9 November. Furthermore, it is well known that reference to the deaths of close friends frightened the superstitious Picasso, and consciously or subconsciously he avoided them. Examples of posthumous representations, either as direct statements or indirect, oblique references, are extremely rare in his work. Casagemas, Manolo, Max Jacob, and possibly Ramon Pichot are the only generally recognized examples.

In October 1939, when a poster was made for an Exhibition at the Bibliothèque Nationale in Paris of Apollinaire's work, it was Picasso's very early humorous drawing, *Apollinaire the Academician*, not recorded in Zervos, that was used rather than any later "tribute."

---

[49]   Lydia GASMAN, *supra* note 12, p. 952, Illustr. 266, 267.

[50]   Lydia GASMAN, *supra* note 12, p.952

Fig.45   *Musical Instrument*, 1925.

Fig.46   *Musical Instrument*, 1925.

Furthermore, when requested to design a monument to Apollinaire, Picasso submitted only his "wire construction" sketches of 1927 and 1928, which were rejected.

A thorough study of all available Picasso works from 1919 to 1970 failed to reveal any November references to Apollinaire; had Picasso paid a belated and mystical tribute in 1925, after seven long years, as Gasman suggests, it was the only time. This view is supported by Pierre Daix who says that although "l'Oiseau du Bénin" proposed three sculptures in memory of Apollinaire, he did not execute any known sketches of him after the poet's death.[51]

Suffice to say, that if we take into account 1) *Musical Instrument*, dated November 1925, signed by Picasso and unmistakably containing Marie-Thérèse's initials; 2) the first "double image" painting dated February 1925, in which the subject strikingly resembles Marie-Thérèse (Fig.24), and which was followed by an unbroken string of such images down to 1938; and 3) Pierre Daix's discovery of the recumbent body of Marie-Thérèse in *Still Life with Musical Instruments*, dated 1925 in Zervos, then Marie-Thérèse's apparently ambiguous remark of October 1977, "Fifty years? It was even longer than that," takes on considerable significance and credibility.

The reticence and secrecy with which Picasso for so long surrounded his affair with Marie-Thérèse are well known, and Picasso's verbal statements about it were unreliable and confusing to say the least. In his *oeuvre*, however, Picasso was remarkably candid and revealing, a characteristic abundantly documented by art historians and critics.

---

[51]   Pierre DAIX, personal communication to André Villers, 15 June 1986, Mougins.

Le Couple Amoureux and Le Couple dans l'Herbe.

In 1974 Marie-Thérèse, reliving memories of her youth and of her great "amour fou," mentioned to me: "Pablo Picasso and I used to hide away from all the people (all the world?) in a secluded spot near the river bank".[52] At that time, I considered this to be a singularly girlish-and touching-remark, coming as it did from a lonely and kind-hearted woman. Marie-Thérèse was still very beautiful, at times eager and revealing, but sadness was written on the face of this woman (Photo 4) who will be remembered in the history of art in the same vein as Goya's "Naked Maja," Rembrandt's Saskia, and Velasquez's "Maria-Teresa," that other "Infanta."

Years later, while searching for clues relative to the "coded" *Musical Instrument* of November 1925 (Fig.44), I came across Picasso's etchings of 17 November 1925 illustrated in Bloch[53].

In the dry-point line etching entitled *Le Couple Amoureux,* a young girl sits by what appears to be a river bank with a man, who is close behind her. His hands, resting on her shoulder, seem to be holding an open book. The man reads; the girl appears to be listening... (Fig.47)

Compare the girl in this etching to the one in *Le Repos du Sculpteur* of March 1933 (Fig.48).

---

[52]   Conversation with Marie-Thérèse Walter, Menton, 1974.

[53]   BLOCH, *supra* note 15 p.38, Pl.71 and 72.

Fig. 47 *Le Couple Amoureux*, dry-point etching, 17 November 1925.

Fig.48 *Le Repos du Sculpteur*, eau-forte, 31 March 1933.

The etching entitled *Le Couple dans l'Herbe* (Fig.49), is more stylized and most beautiful. In it would appear to be the same young girl, with a band around her head; she leans on the shoulder of a man who looks older. Beside him, the man's hat hangs on a walking stick. The man and girl, infinitely suspended in themselves, gaze intently on the swiftly passing water...

Compare the face of the girl in this etching to that of the girl holding a basket of flowers in "The Bearded Painter's Saga" (Fig.12).

A coincidence? An association based on Marie-Thérèse's reminiscence? Maybe so. But if these etchings represent Picasso and Marie-Thérèse, then the two must have known each other <u>before the 17th of November 1925</u>!

These dry-points were pulled in 1961 in a limited edition of 65, but in an unprecedented gesture Picasso kept all the prints for himself! Only in 1983, after the settlement of Picasso's estate, did *Le Couple dans l'Herbe* surface for the first time, at the Galerie Leiris. This work was inspired not only by the stylistic elegance of Manet's *Le Déjeuner sur l'Herbe*, which in the early 1960s Picasso would reinterpret in hundreds of sketches and paintings, but also by Picasso's identification with Manet, who like himself, had accosted a young girl in a busy Parisian thoroughfare, Victorine Meurent, his future mistress and model for that most famous of courtesans "Olympia". In *Le Couple dans l'Herbe* Picasso's *alter ego*, romantically linked with Marie-Thérèse, seems to be none other than the Bearded Painter Édouard Manet!

Add to these works the lithograph *Woman's Head* (Fig.25) with its "double image," also dated November 1925 as we noted earlier and

Fig.49   *Le Couple dans l'Herbe*, dry-point etching, 17 November
1925.

the "double image" sketch from Picasso's carnet No.89[54], signed and dated November 1925, and there emerge as many statements by Picasso of increasing closeness with this "unknown young girl" in the month of November 1925. This analysis is supported by the "coded" *Musical Instrument* of November 1925 (Fig.44) in which Marie-Thérèse's initials are unmistakably represented and by the depiction of "the nude and recumbent Marie-Thérèse" hidden in the *Still Life with Musical Instruments* which also dates from the end of 1925. Thus the *Woman's Head* (Fig.24) of February 1925 is related to a number of other Picassos of that year, works in which there are clear references to Marie-Thérèse. It is no longer an isolated phenomenon. More importantly this "double image" portrait of February 1925, is linked to a large number of similar representations in 1925 and 1926 which in turn merge with a continuous series of such "double images" that dates to the generally acknowledged period of Marie-Thérèse's presence in Picasso's life.

Picasso in these autobiographical statements seems to be saying, "here is the surface, and you must think of or rather feel intuitively what lies beneath it, because everything I touch comes to life and becomes the incarnation of some aspect of my internal drama". We must not take Picasso too literally, however. His fantasies and dreams played a part in his romantic and erotic statements, as did, frequently, accidental objects, personages, and disguises.

Keeping in mind the complexity of Picasso the image maker, I was well aware that there were pitfalls inherent in following such an intricate pathway. Nonetheless, on the basis of Jung's concept of "synchronicity", that is meaningful correspondence of encounters, chance happenings, and of my comparative analysis of Picasso's work from 1925 to 1927, I began to uncover the hidden story of Picasso's relationship with Marie-Thérèse, which I had strong reasons to believe had commenced long before January the 8th 1927...

---

54   Arnold and Marc GLIMCHER, *supra* note 39, p.325

L'Atelier de la Modiste, January 1926,
(The Milliner's Workshop).

I have assumed justifiably, I believe, that Picasso's art is autobiographical, a private diary so to speak, which anyone familiar with Picasso could usually read. At the same time, to make such a statement is to underestimate the complexity of Picasso, and as if to point that out to us, he confounds us in one of his most important paintings. I refer here to his great curvilinear cubist composition: *L'Atelier de la Modiste* of January 1926 (Fig.50). According to my analysis, this work, for which he had made a number of studies in Carnets No.88, 89 and 90[55]., fell within the framework of his production issuing from the liaison that he had already established with Marie-Thérèse. However, I had no evidence that Marie-Thérèse or her mother, Émilie Marguerite had ever worked in a milliner's shop.

Still, in view of my assumption about the autobiographical nature of Picasso's work, I felt there had to be an answer to this riddle, and that I had none, bothered me a great deal.

L'Atelier de la Modiste, this large and complicated composition, was finished early in January 1926, which suggests that Picasso had started it in 1925. According to Pierre Daix, Picasso painted it from his fourth-floor studio window, situated directly opposite the actual

---

[55]   Arnold and Marc GLIMCHER, *supra* note 39.

Fig.50   *L'Atelier de la Modiste*, oil on canvas, January 1926.

workshop on rue La Boétie.[56] In this connection it is worth quoting Rosalind Krauss's pertinent observation: "Not least of all, we must consider the anomalous nature of the work's subject, in a long period otherwise entirely barren of anything we could call genre painting..." that Picasso could translate "the idea of three little shop girls at work in their saleroom, a subject right out of Degas seems curious to say the least".[57]

However, *L'Atelier de la Modiste* contains references transcending Krauss's "three little shop girls." And as I pointed out in the study of the significance of Picasso's "double images," those images, so intimately connected to Marie-Thérèse, had for Picasso associations of extraordinary significance. Their presence <u>in this one painting in no less than three personages,</u> namely the two younger girls, and the older woman, in edition to Picasso himself at the door of the Atelier, would suggest, therefore, some association with an actual event. But who were these people, and what was Picasso doing in a milliner's workshop? By 1926, Picasso's marriage had deteriorated to such an extent that clearly he was not there to buy his wife Olga a pretty hat, and this conclusion seems particularly clear if we note that the seated girl on the left side of the picture resembles Marie-Thérèse in the *Sculptural Sketches* (Fig.5) and paintings of 1926-27!

In time I became absolutely convinced that something significant was hidden behind the shop doors that the elderly woman is opening, something that had eluded me and had important bearing on my study. But would it be still possible to retrace Marie-Thérèse's steps after so many years, assuming, as I did, that it was indeed she who was in that mysterious atelier? This of course I did not know. The prospect did not seem hopeful since the only clue I had was that in the

---

[56]   Pierre DAIX, *Picasso*, New York, Praeger, 1965, p.134

[57]   Rosalind E. KRAUSS, *The Sketchbooks of Picasso*, London, Thames and Hudson Ltd., 1986, p.116

104

mid 1920s, sixty years before to be exact, Marie-Thérèse had lived with her mother at "Maisons Alfort" on the outskirts of Paris, and "Maisons Alfort" sounded like the name of a large apartment house!

A few weeks later I landed in France. The Paris Metro took me to Maisons Alfort, a large bustling town on the River Marne.

Picasso and Marie-Thérèse Walter

1925-1927

Part 2

France

6 cité d'Alfort
Maisons Alfort
8-28 October 1986.

It was not an easy task to reconstruct the story of Picasso and Marie-Thérèse after more than sixty years.

Much on the controversial Picasso, even in the mid-twenties, was well known and documented, and what I did not know, I gathered from his associates and friends.

But of his teen-aged Juliet, I knew little, and even of that was less than certain. Her origins were obscure. Her father may have been a painter on skidrow, having simply abandoned his family and disappeared.

In "Picasso and Marie-Thérèse Walter", John Richardson refers to her mother, Émilie-Marguerite, as being Swedish or of partly Swedish origin, "which explains her daughter's striking Scandinavian looks"[58].. He disagrees with Pierre Cabanne who stated that Émilie Marguerite was Swiss...

In fact on my arrival in France, the pertinent information I had on Marie-Thérèse Walter was scanty or based on undocumented hearsay. The only solid fact I had was that Marie-Thérèse was born at Perreux-sur-Marne in 1909, and that in the 1920s she lived for a number of years with her mother at Maisons Alfort. Thus, it seemed reasonable to start my inquiries there.

---

[58]   John RICHARDSON, *supra* note 13, p.66

In those days long ago when Picasso first met Marie-Thérèse, Maisons Alfort must have been a tranquil suburb of villas, ancient cottages, fields, and orchards, strung along the river. Today, owing to its close proximity to Paris, it is an endless vista of apartment buildings, industrial complexes, crowded boulevards, and streets, divided by the concrete embankments of the Marne and numerous overpasses over which trains rush by.

After many days at the Departmental Archives, I discovered that the villa occupied by Émilie Marguerite in the 1920s still existed at 6 cité d'Alfort, a tiny street located between the busy boulevard General Leclerc and an embankment of the Marne. It had probably been saved from destruction by the complexities of the legal system; following the death of Émilie Marguerite in 1946, it had passed into the hands of her only son, and after his death in 1971 no fewer than 11 persons laid claim to it. This old villa would serve as my spring board to delve into the past, for the titles to it had been meticulously preserved in the Departmental Archives for the Districts of Seine and Marne. From it I painstakingly pursued my endless search for the mysterious *Atelier de la Modiste*, which I was absolutely convinced existed in reality. Gradually the information I was searching for came to light, and with it the story of the "Atelier"...

On the 15th of October 1986, in a small, narrow street not far from the River Marne, I looked for the first time on the villa at 6 cité d'Alfort.

The villa must have been a lovely place once, but now it was a sad and depressing sight. Behind a stone wall and an iron gate, it stood deserted and decaying, not wanting to be disturbed, its garden overgrown with weeds. Inquiries on the street brought no information about the Walter family. The last occupant of the villa was an unknown elderly lady, now senile and living in a hospital. The place had been unoccupied for a considerable time, but the old man who looked after the garden was still alive and perhaps, it was suggested, he would have the information I was searching for...

I found him. He had lived in the neighbourhood since 1950 but had never heard of either Émilie Marguerite or Marie-Thérèse Walter. I was just about to turn away when in a sudden flash of inspiration I asked: "Picasso. Have you ever heard mention of Picasso?" His puzzled face came to life: "Picasso? Why, yes! The old lady whose garden I was taking care of, spoke to my wife of Picasso." "So she knew Picasso!?" "No, I don't think so, but her relatives did. Apparently he used to come here sometime before the war."

He gave me the name of the last occupant of the villa. Puzzled I ponder over that name; it did not suggest a French origin. Nonetheless, this old lady's relatives had a knowledge of Picasso, and according to what she told to the gardener's wife, Picasso visited the villa before the war.

So there must have been some connection between her relatives and the Walter family. The entire network of my Picasso friends and collaborators studied the name, but no one knew it. Fed to the data banks on Picasso and Marie-Thérèse, the name produced empty results on the screens: "Searching" and then "Inconnu", "Unknown"... It seemed as if my efforts to trace the pale ghosts of the past would end in vain.

It is 11 pm October the 16th. Pulled by some invisible force I stand again in front of the deserted villa at 6 cité d'Alfort. It is only a few steps from the River Marne, haunting and mysterious, and once more, out of the distant past I hear the voice of Marie-Thérèse echoing in the silent street: "Pablo Picasso and I used to meet on the deserted river bank." The place could not have been far from here! Her kind, deeply lined face and beautiful sad eyes cast a pale shadow of remembrance... How incredibly lonely had been the journey of this woman beside that of the world-famous Picasso, "whose hands could create and destroy"!

The suicide of Jacqueline Picasso.

In the face of Marie-Thérèse's tragedy I am filled with a sense of foreboding. These dark Picassian forces seem to me totally incomprehensible. Yesterday, when I tried to call Jacqueline Picasso at Notre-Dame-de-Vie, the phone had rung emptily time and time again...[59]

Like a mute sentinel I stand in front of this deserted villa suspended between the world of the dead and the world of the living with the ghosts of Picasso, Marie-Thérèse and now Jacqueline whispering in the dark.

I am compelled by a strange premonition to wait.

A feeble lamp illuminates the darkness of the narrow street. A man steps out into the pool of light it creates; he is walking his dog. I recognize him as the man who used to look after this garden... Surprised to see me he silently approaches and hands me a piece of paper. "I got the name from my wife." It is the same family name as the baffling one, of the old lady who lived here, and which in the light of my previous inquiries proved to be of no consequence. But this time, on the piece of paper, beside the name, a telephone number of this lady's close relative is also there.

---

[59] I refer here to my attempts to reach Jacqueline Picasso at Notre-Dame-de-Vie on the morning of the 15th October 1986; the day of her suicide.

Marie-Thérèse Walter: the Franco-Swedish connection.

It was through this lady's relative, blue eyed and fair, that I was able to reconstruct the complex affairs of men and women, the pleasure loving Parisians of *la belle époque*, whose lives would relate directly to the work in progress.

My informant was not only acquainted with the history of his Franco-Swedish family going back to the reign of Louis XIII, but, he was also aware of many of its incidental details, including the love affair of one of his senior relatives.   The scant description of it here, barely touches the surface of this complicated affair, which even to this day is a closely guarded family secret.

It was in the early 1900s that this informant's relative was in love with his secretary and confidante of many years.

This woman was Émilie Marguerite.

An impoverished painter, who had abandoned Émilie Marguerite, as has been repeated with monotonous regularity in monographs on Marie-Thérèse?   On the contrary, he was a highly accomplished individual, whose products are household names in all of France.   And at the time of his liaison with Émilie Marguerite, this "foresaken painter" was one of the richest and influential businessmen in Paris!!   He saw to it that his two oldest daughters with Émilie Marguerite were educated in one of the most exclusive lycea in Paris, studied medicine at the Sorbonne, and qualified as doctors;   in later years they were highly regarded as specialists in their field.   There is no need for the purpose of my study to elaborate on this relationship, but there can be no doubt that this man cared for Émilie Marguerite, and assisted her for as long as he could.

As one of his children, Marie-Thérèse was fair, blue-eyed, and strikingly beautiful. In her early teens, she ripened into a voluptuous Aphrodite, yet there was an aura about her of great innocence and purity. Wherever she went, she cast a strange spell on people; they could not help but turn and stare at her.

*Brief genealogical and historical considerations of
the Émilie-Marguerite Walter family.*

Quite recently, through a thorough genealogical investigation and interviews in France, I obtained a number of hitherto unknown facts concerning Marie-Thérèse Walter and her relationship with Pablo Picasso.

Marie-Thérèse was the grand daughter of Burkard Frederic Walter, born in Heidelberg, Germany, on 20 February 1833. To avoid military service in Germany he had moved to France, first living in Montparnasse, and later at Maisons Alfort. In time, he became a wealthy plumbing contractor and entrepreneur, but he had to flee France during the Franco-Prussian War. With the German Army advancing on Paris, he managed to escape across the English Channel in a balloon. For a while he lived in London, and returned to France after the cessation of hostilities.

On the 1 May 1891 he became a naturalized French citizen, and for a number of years his name appeared on the electoral register at Maisons Alfort. He had two children, Émilie Marguerite Walter born in Paris on 22 May 1871, and a son Aristide Émile Walter, born also there in 1873.

Some time in the early 1900s, Burkard Frederic Walter married for the fourth time.On this occasion his bride was the sister of his daughter's husband. Émilie Marguerite was married at the time to a Victor Schwarz, a drunkard who abused her; they had no children, and after a few years their marriage was dissolved.

After this Émilie Marguerite Walter had four children with a Frenchman of Swedish extraction, whose ancestors had settled in France at the time of Louis XIII as lumbermen and carpenters to assist in building the French fleet. Émilie Marguerite's children were: a son born in 1903; a daughter born the following year; another daughter born in 1906, and Marie-Thérèse, born in 1909 at Perreux-sur-Marne, not far from Maisons Alfort. Since at that time women did not have the right to vote, Émilie Marguerite's name appeared only in the census register of Maisons Alfort. In 1926-27, she became the proprietor of 6 cité d'Alfort apparently by inheritance from her father. The legacy is curious because Walter's last wife was apparently still alive as was his son Aristide Émile. Émilie Marguerite Walter appeared in the census of Maisons Alfort in 1931 as "divorced" with one daughter, Marie-Thérèse; she had no known occupation. In 1936 she was listed as "married," with two daughters. Her son had moved out in 1931, and, following his mother's death in 1946, he inherited the house.

In the 1920s, Marie-Thérèse's sisters were studying in Paris. Later they joined the faculty of medicine and lived with relatives in the city, while the younger girl stayed with her mother, at 6 cité d'Alfort. After the First World War, Marie-Thérèse with Émilie Marguerite had spent time in Wiesbaden, Germany, not far from Heidelberg, where Émilie Marguerite had relatives.

You must not always believe
what I say.
Questions tempt you to tell lies,
particularly when there is no
answer.

Picasso

Picasso's first meeting with Marie-Thérèse Walter.
Gare St-Lazare, Paris 1925.

As suggested by the pictorial evidence presented in this study and by an autobiographical interpretation of Picasso's work, I had strong reasons to believe that the famous meeting between Picasso and Marie-Thérèse Walter had occurred long before the 8th of January 1927. Acting on intuition, since the time I was confronted by Picasso's sketch *The Seated Girl*, 1926 and on an exhaustive study of Picasso's work for 1925-1927, I managed to gather formidable evidence in support of this possibility. The genealogical inquiry and interviews confirmed the hypothesis suggested by my original research.

One day Picasso, who lived on rue La Boétie, not far from Galeries Lafayette, saw Marie-Thérèse, accompanied by her older sister, walk out of that department store. Dumbstruck by Marie-Thérèse, he followed the two girls to the Gare St.Lazare, where Marie-Thérèse was to catch the train to Maisons Alfort. There, as we have pointed out before, she was living with her mother, Émilie Marguerite, while her older sister was living and studying in the city. Since the two sisters were extremely fond of each other, they were loath to part and embraced time and time again, giggling and laughing, while the fascinated Picasso punched a hole in the newspaper he was carrying to watch them unobserved![60] Finally, the older sister had

---

[60] Later Picasso would tease Marie-Thérèse about how well this stratagem had worked, since he was able to accost her alone after the older sister had left.

to part, and it was then that Picasso accosted the young Marie-Thérèse, and with great urgency expressed his desire to see her again. Cold and aloof, Marie-Thérèse completely ignored the "Old Man," turned away from him. Picasso was beside himself. Flushed and agitated he grabbed her by the arm, and exclaimed: "Miss, I shall wait for you here every evening at 6 pm. I must see you again!"

Some time later, Marie-Thérèse confided in her sister about the incident at the railway station. Amused and curious, the two girls went to Gare St.Lazare at 6 pm to see if the "Old Man" was there. He was. Sitting on the bench, patiently waiting and reading his newspaper! For several days the two sisters watched him unobserved, until one day unable to refrain her curiosity, the older sister urged Marie-Thérèse: "Go on and talk to him!" Which she did. And this happened a considerable time before January of 1927. She was still very much of a teenager in 1925, when "Pic" (Picasso's nickname in the Walter 's family) followed the two sisters to Gare St.Lazare."[61]

Picasso got into the habit of picking up Marie-Thérèse at 6 cité d'Alfort and taking her to amusement parks, movies, or secret rendez-vous beside the Marne. He became very fond of her mother and identified his "paternal

---

Interviews in France, October 1986.

[61] This narrative was given to me by an older sister of Marie-Thérèse, a physician of unquestionable integrity. There were no "leading questions" asked relative to Marie-Thérèse, since the main purpose of this visit was to gather information about the Walter family. So whatever information was obtained concerning Marie-Thérèse, was given spontaneously and freely. Although this older sister described Marie-Thérèse as "keeping things to herself and being secretive", undoubtedly she was aware of the reasons for the secrecy, namely Picasso's physical relationship with her teen-aged sister.
But as the myth of that famous meeting of the 8th January 1927 became part of Picassian history, she upbraided Marie-Thérèse for her sister's unwarranted secrecy so long after the event!

incestuous" feelings towards Marie-Thérèse with Émilie Marguerite's "maternal" instinct.

And since Picasso was not Picasso when he could not paint, in due course, he installed a studio in the old shed at the back of the spacious garden at 6 cité d'Alfort, where, protected by the high walls surrounding the beautifully kept garden, he could paint undisturbed.

Recently, some brushes belonging to Picasso were found in this shed.

*Reference to Photo 1- Marie-Thérèse Walter
as a teen-ager.*

The well known studio photo, supposedly taken in 1927, of a young Marie-Thérèse, sitting on a stone wall, wearing a wide brimmed felt hat before a background that included a pseudo-Gothic cupola and suggestive of a mineral spring enclosure, then popular in Europe (Photo 1 Maya Ruiz Picasso coll.) was in fact taken in Wiesbaden, Germany on the 20 October 1922, when Marie-Thérèse was 13 years old[62].

Also, the first pencil sketches Picasso did of Marie-Thérèse (Maya Ruiz Picasso coll.) supposedly done in "the Spring of 1927" should be re-examined with an earlier date in mind.

---

[62] In 1974, while visiting Marie-Thérèse, I saw the original photo (Photo 1) of Marie-Thérèse and it was unmistakably dated 20th October 1922! In 1922, when the older sister of Marie-Thérèse visited her mother Émilie Marguerite in Wiesbaden, Germany, she had her photo taken at the same time as Marie-Thérèse; she also was wearing a beautiful felt hat.

Les Modistes, January 1926.

Perhaps the most important aspect of this essay for the art historian is that it presents the relationship between Picasso and Marie-Thérèse from a new perspective and consequently gives us added insight into Picasso's art.

AUTOBIOGRAPHICAL. During Picasso's liaison with Marie-Thérèse, the courtship, the passionate period, and the decline, Picasso's art is thoroughly autobiographical. And no matter how assiduously Picasso tried to hide it in his painting, the truth was always there, and in the end it invariably comes out. An example is provided by one of his most important paintings of that period, *L'Atelier de la Modiste*, or *The Milliner's Workshop*, January 1926 (Fig.50); it <u>is inaccurately titled</u>, because this mysterious *Atelier* never existed!

Who gave the work that title, I do not know, but it has stuck and the myth of an atelier has persisted over the years, aided no doubt by the ambiguous nature of the painting itself. And Picasso, being Picasso, did not give a damn for such a mundane thing as the title given by art historians to one of his paintings. In fact, in view of the secrecy that he wished to maintain around his affair with Marie-Thérèse, he was probably wickedly pleased!

The search for a non-existent atelier led me astray for a considerable time. Picasso's own title for the painting was <u>*LES MODISTES*</u>,, and earlier in this essay, I noted the close relationship between it and his "Sculptural Sketches" of 1925-6, the subject of which bore striking resemblance to Marie-Thérèse.

It must have been one of Picasso's first visits to 6 cité d'Alfort; he enters through the partly glassed door[63] as Émilie Marguerite opens it for him, and announces his arrival to Marie-Thérèse, who, with her sister, is busy making the broad rimmed felt hats they were so fond of! Marie-Thérèse raises one eye towards the visitor... Note Picasso's "double image" on Émilie Marguerite's face. In *Les Modistes*, Émilie Marguerite forms the authoritative central part, while the shadowy substance of Picasso, enclosing her in a "magic mask" attempts to propitiate her spirit. The partly open door, with its huge knob, is Picasso's symbol for the future. Since the consequences of this highly significant visit were not lost on Picasso, he also endowed Marie-Thérèse and her sister with his magic "double images," thus predicting profound changes in this young girl's placid existence at Maisons Alfort, and setting the stage in motion for one of his most dramatic plays, faithfully recorded, act by act, scene by scene, in his amazing Journals, from its dizzying erotic heights until its prophetic final tragedy[64]. *Les Modistes* is Picasso's greatest expression of the free flowing curvilinear cubism. In fabricating the myth that he had met Marie-Thérèse on 8 January 1927, Picasso dealt her a mean blow for he denied her presence in one of his finest paintings!

---

63   At the entrance of the villa at 6 cité d'Alfort, there are in fact two doors, a wooden exterior door and a glassed one inside.

64   Soon after their meeting, Marie-Thérèse told Picasso about a young fellow who was in love with one of her sisters. He had threatened to hang himself if the sister did not reciprocate his feelings. Picasso, apparently forgetting his own recent frustration by Marie-Thérèse, did a "comical cartoon" of the unfortunate suitor, which showed him in an aroused sexual state. Alas, the suitor had already hanged himself! Marie-Thérèse gave this sketch to her sister, who, greatly disgusted, tore it up. For Marie-Thérèse who had taken it all as a joke, this picture proved to be a bad omen.

The Hobby Horse , 7 February 1926 (Fig.51), described in the Picasso family archives as "Picasso with his son Paulo" commemorates an outing with Marie-Thérèse that must have had special significance for Picasso.[65]

[65]   During Picasso's visits at 6 cité d'Alfort, Émilie Marguerite was fond of showing the painter an album containing early photos of Marie-Thérèse. Note that in *The Hobby Horse*, 7 February 1926, the seated figure is holding a book (a photo album?) with the inverted initials M.T. Chronologically this work follows closely *Les Modistes* completed in January 1926.

At times Picasso portrayed Marie-Thérèse as a high-spirited white pony with a fringed mane and quizzical facial expression.

Note also on the right side of the sketch, Picasso's "secret cabinet," with the "P"-like key, in which he kept his erotica and intimate correspondence, and, at the back, a large mirror identical to one sketched by Picasso in his Studio at rue de la Boétie in 1920 (illustrated in André FERMIGIER, *Picasso*, Paris, Librairie Hachette, p.25).

Fig.51   *The Hobby Horse*, china ink, 7 February 1926.

And the magnificent series of *Girls Reading* (Fig.52, Z-VIII-190, 191, 192, 194) Boisgeloup, March 1934, were of Marie-Thérèse and an older dark-haired sister, who used to visit there frequently.[66]

---

66   Picasso tried to remedy Marie-Thérèse's lack of formal education by giving the girl books. Note in *Girls Reading* the passive and bored look of the younger, fair haired girl (Marie-Thérèse) and the more authoritative, concentrated expression of her dark-haired, older, well educated sister.

Fig.52   *Girls Reading*, oil on canvas, 1934.

Discussion

On the basis of biographical information gleaned from Picasso's works, documentary evidence, and information obtained from members of Marie-Thérèse's family, I shall attempt to reconstruct the sequence of events following Picasso's first encounter with Marie-Thérèse. The difficulties and pitfalls inherent in trying to recreate events after such a considerable period of time, and in trying to cast light on a liaison that had for so long been carefully kept in darkness are obvious. A particular problem was a scarcity of works by Picasso for the first part of 1925 referring directly to Marie-Thérèse; there are only two works with "double images" of subjects bearing a striking resemblance to Marie-Thérèse, namely those of February and July 1925 (Fig.24 and 34). However, for the period July-December 1925 there are no less than 38 such images! This sudden production is not surprising, because with Picasso the seed of an aesthetic idea took a long time to germinate; numerous examples of this slow maturation exist in connection with Picasso's well known and documented female partners. Picasso's "double image" studies from February until July 1925, though few in number, are not his only indications of his knowledge of Marie-Thérèse. His works dated July 1925, express his conscious or subconscious unease, and appear to be indirectly related to Marie-Thérèse. These highly important, seemingly "unconnected fragments" of Picassos will be discussed later in this chapter.

Picasso was truthful in stating that he saw Marie-Thérèse Walter for the first time in front of the Galeries Lafayette, but he omitted to say that she was not alone, and that in following her to Gare St. Lazare, where he accosted her, he had awaited the departure of her sister[67]. From my analysis of *Woman's Head* (Fig.24) I judged that this event had occurred early in 1925, and this conclusion was later confirmed by Marie-Thérèse's relative. Although dated 1924 on the front , the painting contains, on the back, an explanatory note in Picasso's hand: "Started in 1924, finished in February 1925" Thus, one might hazard a guess that his encounter with Marie-Thérèse occurred in January or February of that year, and that after a lapse of probably no more than two or three weeks, Marie-Thérèse, full of curiosity and urged on by her sister, approached the "Old Man" and spoke to him.

After reviewing the data discussed in Parts I and II of this study, I cannot accept as valid the supposition that Picasso had "prefigured Marie-Thérèse by several years" before the legendary meeting of January 1927. In the earliest representation of Marie-Thérèse known to me, that of February 1925, (Fig.24), Picasso not only "prefigured" her classic Nordic face, tension and introspection, but also, in this likeness of Marie-Thérèse is the first representation of Picasso's "double image," a totally new technique in his oeuvre, by which Picasso's own profile is traced on the lateral aspect of the girl's face. These "double images," unique to the period of Picasso's relationship with Marie-Thérèse, as indicated in the first chapter of this study, will increase in number, and those of the period before 1927 will merge into the long series produced in the period in which it is acknowledged that Picasso had relations with Marie-Thérèse. Picasso continued to produce "double images" until his relationship with Marie-Thérèse declined (Graph1).

After that first meeting, sometime in the first two months of 1925, Picasso, in one of his characteristic moves to get away from the woman he wanted[68] accompanied Olga and little Paulo to Monte-Carlo in March 1925. He returned to Paris in May. It is not known if he saw

---

67   *supra* note 60

68   I refer here to similar episodes with Dora Maar, Françoise Gilot, Geneviève Laporte, and Jacqueline Picasso.

Marie-Thérèse on his return, he probably did. But according to family sources, Marie-Thérèse kept the "Old Man" at a distance for some time, "exhibiting a great deal of nonchalance and independence." Marie-Thérèse later told her daughter Maya that "it was only after 6 months that Papa took Mama by the hand." Shy, flushed, boyish, and eager, extremely conscious and jealous of the impression the teen-aged Marie-Thérèse created on younger men, Picasso did his utmost to please her by taking her to the movies, fairs, and circuses to gain her friendship and dependency on him. It is obvious that had anything of importance happened during this period, Picasso being Picasso, he would surely have "recorded" it the way that he did later.

These observations, however, run contrary to John Richardson's[69] interpretation of Picasso's early relationship with Marie-Thérèse, based on the extensive interviews Lydia Gasman had with Marie-Thérèse in December 1971 and January 1972, and on his "personal knowledge of Picasso." Richardson concludes that Picasso deflowered Marie-Thérèse soon after they met.

This may have been the case, but in retrospect it seems most unlikely. Richardson himself quotes Marie-Thérèse's repeated assertions that "no intimacy took place until at least 6 months after our first meeting, when he asked me to pose for him in the nude". Whether she was referring to their first encounter at Gare St.Lazare, or to the first real meeting later, we do not know. The fact remains, that after laying herself bare as Picasso's "Femme Enfant," and doing her utmost to convince Gasman that she had been his greatest love, Marie-Thérèse had every reason to confirm an early intimacy had there indeed been one. Judging from the highly intimate nature of her interviews with Gasman, there was little that she left hidden.

Little is known about the young Marie-Thérèse; I obtained only a few revealing glimpses of her personality from a close relative. During my brief encounter with Marie-Thérèse in 1974 she did indeed

---

[69]   John RICHARDSON, *supra* note 13, p.3

live in the past, but that past was only in relation to Picasso and was not a clear reflection of herself.

But if our knowledge of Marie-Thérèse is meagre, the same cannot be said of Picasso, whose personality and sexual habits are documented in amazing detail. We know, for example, that his *modus operandi* with women was surprisingly repetitive.

Basically, Picasso was shy, but he was also vain and conscious of his worth. He was extremely devious in his ways, and making up his mind was a long, painful process; he procrastinated endlessly. "Que no haya nonedad" was his motto: "may no new things arise"; in Picasso's idiom that meant: "let me and my work go undisturbed." We are not implying here that Picasso purposely avoided women, on the contrary. He was very much conscious of them, and in his life, including of course his sexual life, painting and women were inseparably linked. Women were the springboard of Picasso's imagination. But he was not a "physical" man, given to spontaneous physical impulses as were those matadors[70], and athletes whom he envied and admired.

Picasso above all was a cerebral lover, and Picasso's biggest sex organ was his brain. It endowed him with boundless erotic imagination, which he employed with great success in his work, but it also made him rationalize and procrastinate before fully committing himself. And he usually did not commit himself until, aided by "propitious circumstances," he had managed to manoeuvre his partner into a subservient position and to establish a relationship on his own terms. It is quite clear from Picasso's history, that from the time of his liaison with Fernande Olivier, this process took months or even years

---

[70]   Eugène ARIAS, Picasso's barber and friend, in conversation with me in 1985, quoted Picasso as saying, "You know Arias, when we conduct beautiful tall women to their seats in the arena, we are like Picadors, merely pricking their breasts with the "pics" of our elbows [Picasso and Arias were just over 5 feet in height]. It takes a powerful matador, with a sword, to deliver the "coup de grâce".

to accomplish. This characteristic fits badly into the Picassian myth of a man of countless adventures, and exploits with women, a legend that Picasso was at great pains to propagate. Thus an "early deflowering" of Marie-Thérèse would not be in keeping with the nature of the man.

Furthermore, for much of 1925 Picasso was a man beset with problems. He badly wanted Marie-Thérèse. He was obsessed with her; of that there can't be any doubt. But if she was the "Femme-Enfant" of the Surrealists come true, she was a "Femme-Enfant" nevertheless, and ever since his involvement with the Iberian statues stolen from the Louvre, Picasso had entertained the healthiest respect for the French judiciary. He must have been aware that to embark on an affair such as this one, he had to be assured of the complicity not only of Marie-Thérèse, but also of her mother and other members of the Walter family. That could not have been achieved overnight.

And there was Olga, his wife, a jealous, possessive, and tyrannical woman, who made his life hell. One can only surmise what his feelings were, when, in July of 1925 he and Olga embarked once more on their pilgrimage to fashionable Juan-les-Pins! At Juan-les-Pins, with Olga on his back, dragging him from one social function to another, Picasso was desperate. Tormented by sexual longings, enraged, empty, insecure, and powerless, bound to Olga by Paulo and the chains of marriage, Picasso paints. Painting is the safety valve which keeps him on an even keel. And, with a painter like Picasso, sooner or later these emotions will be reflected in his work. Anyone looking at Picasso's Juan-les-Pins paintings of 1925, can see quite clearly the state of agitation that he was in. And yet, in spite of profound dissatisfaction with himself and life in general, Picasso exerts iron will and discipline to control his emotions, bend them to his will, and present them in paint as autobiographical statements!

The Cage
(Fig.53)

Symbolically depicting Picasso's helpless state under Olga's domination is *The Cage* (Fig.53). By a terraced window, with a free view of the sky, a forlorn and bedraggled bird sits in a cage and looks at a double headed sculpture of two women, one dark, one fair. Choleric, with widely open beak, the little bird seems to be reproaching the dark headed woman for his captivity. She fixes it with an uncompromising stare; the head of the fair woman less prominent, looks anxiously on this scene.

Undoubtedly, this work reflects Picasso's stifled existence with Olga on the fashionable Côte d'Azur; like a bird in the gilded cage he is unable to escape.

Observe Picasso's similar thematic representation in *Birds in the Cage*, 1937 (Fig.19).

Fig.53 *The Cage*, oil on canvas, Juan-les-Pins, July 1925.

The Studio with the Plaster Head,
(Fig.54)

Closely related to *The Cage* in spirit, *The Studio with the Plaster Head* describes Picasso's emotional paralysis at Juan-les-Pins. In this work Picasso holds a dialogue with himself, or rather with his *alter ego*, "The Bearded Painter", represented here as "Plaster Head" in profile. Terrified, the statue looks at himself with anguished eye: he is all in pieces, his limbs, broken and disjointed lie scattered in the studio, an explicit reference to Picasso's emotional paralysis and indecision, since without limbs he cannot move. From the side of the "Plaster Head", projects the barely visible part of a woman's head, the obvious cause of the artist's torment and distress.

Behind the head of the statue is its shadow, from one side of which an ear-like door-knob can be seen; perhaps a reference to Picasso's own dark and uncertain future.

Fig.54 *The Studio with the Plaster Head*, oil on canvas, Juan-les-Pins, July 1925.

La Statuaire
(Fig.55)

In this work Picasso continues his sombre dialogue, but this time he addresses himself directly to the woman on the side of his head in Fig.54, the woman who obsesses him. Her striking resemblance to Marie-Thérèse is represented in this picture by a young sculptress. Picasso's own presence, obvious, in heavy black, is intertwined with that of this very young woman, a counter to his own advancing years, while he points out to her the future[71], that relentless flow of time of which he, so much older is beholden hostage. To bridge this gap, he reconstructs the drama of her destiny, depicted here in a tragic, white marble head, an uncanny commentary on Marie-Thérèse's later years, which the young girl does not wish to see, and she averts her face from it. *La Statuaire* , 1925, Fig. 55 and Photo 4; Marie-Thérèse Walter, Menton 1974.

Compare the likeness of the sculptress's face with Picasso's "double image" in *Woman's Head* of February 1925 (Fig.24).

---

71   Represented here by a doorknob, projecting from his forehead.

140

Fig.55   *La Statuaire*, oil on canvas, Juan-les-Pins, July 1925.

Photo 4 Marie-Thérèse Walter, Menton 1974.
Luc and Lala Joubert.

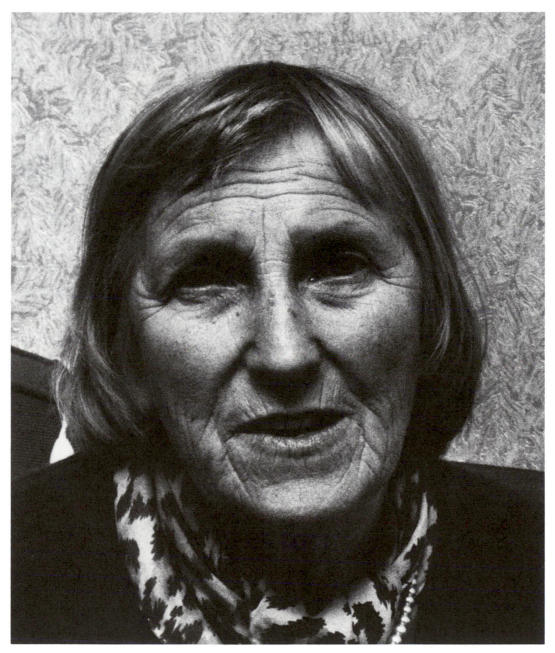

The Embrace [72]
(Fig.56)

     Picasso could not control Marie-Thérèse, and she would obsess him, haunt him and cause him misery and pain, then he would exorcise her power by obliterating her sex. In the throes of rage and sexual frustration he paints *The Embrace* 1925 (Fig.56), his most explicit and brutal sexually oriented work. In it two monsters embrace tightly, the reptile jaws of one, about to devour the mouth of the other, passive, in the form of a gaping vaginal orifice!

---

[72]   The title that Picasso gave to Sabartès for this painting was, *On the Beach*.

Fig.56 *The Embrace*, oil on canvas, Juan-les-Pins, July 1925.

The Dancers
(Fig.57)

The curiously charged dialogue Picasso has with himself, as he vents his rage on the past, the present, and an uncertain future, as well as on the friends and women he once had, continues in the frenzy of *The Dancers* (Fig.57).

Picasso started work on this painting early in 1925, before the death of his estranged friend Ramon Pichot. Undoubtedly affected by that event Picasso incorporated into the painting in progress his reaction to the death.

According to Daix, *The Dancers* was a projection of Picasso's guilt for the death of Pichot.[73] Picasso claimed that he was responsible, for between 1903 and 1905 he had had relations with Germaine, Pichot's wife, and, as Picasso himself said, "this is what's killed him!" Picasso informed Penrose who acquired *The Dancers* for The Tate in London, that he called the work "The Death of Ramon Pichot".[74]

Perhaps. But one should keep in mind that Germaine Pichot was notorious for her numerous affairs with Picasso's friends. The friend he took her from was Manolo, not Pichot!

Nevertheless, after Pichot's death, Picasso supported Germaine financially into old age, and yet refused to do so for his more important

---

[73]   Pierre DAIX, *supra* note 56

[74]   Roland PENROSE, *Picasso- His Life and Work*, London, Granada Publishing, 1981, p.250

Fig.57 *The Dancers*, oil on canvas, 1925.

mistress Fernande Olivier![75] Germaine (née Gargallo) and Ramon Pichot had one daughter, Pierrette, who, observing the Spanish custom, retained her mother's maiden name, Gargallo. In 1963 Josep Palau i Fabre had an interview with Pierrette Gargallo during which she denied being related to the Pichots[76] The nature of the relationship Picasso maintained with Germaine for so many years after their short liaison remains obscure to this day.

In *The Dancers*, on the extreme right of the painting, Picasso's dark silhouette appears in a "double image," the second figure of which appears inside the silhouette. This figure has its head agonizingly thrown back, one eye blind. Picasso's silhouette extends its arm to the frenzied Bacchante on the extreme left. In the centre, with arms upraised, a taller, younger looking dancer balances and joins the dark silhouette to the frenzied Bacchante on the left.

Whether this dancer represents Germaine Pichot in her younger days, Marie-Thérèse, or even Olga, no one knows. However, she is standing in front of a partly opened door with a large knob, Picasso's symbolic representation of the future.

In 1925 Picasso stands on the threshold of cataclysmic changes that will affect his future. They start with his rapidly deteriorating relationship with Olga, and continues with his savage break from the niceties of neo-classicism. Reflected in the frenzy of *The Dancers*, his iconoclastic energy will be carried to the extreme in the *Musical Instruments*, 1926, which are made of coarse rags and projecting sharp nails!

Picasso becomes subject to rages, fearful dreams, and deep depressions. There are long, unexplained absences from Villa Belle-

---

[75]   It should be pointed out that Picasso did help Fernande Olivier during a protracted illness. Author's conversations with Jacqueline Picasso, 1984-85.

[76]   Personal communication, Josep Palau i Fabre, 1987.

Rose at Juan-les-Pins...[77]   It is fairly certain that he painted *The Cage* (Fig.53), *Studio with the Plaster Head* (Fig.54), *La Statuaire* (Fig.55), and *The Embrace* (Fig.56) while there with Olga in July 1925.   However, his movements on the Riviera in August are poorly documented— and what information there is, can be obtained only indirectly from his sketch-books or Carnets, which until recently were unpublished.

---

[77]   Patrick O'BRIAN, *Pablo Ruiz Picasso*, Paris, Gallimard, 1979, p.343

Picasso's sketch-books (carnets).

Carnet No.87[78] finishes on 1 August 1925. Carnet No.88[79] is inscribed, on its front cover, "Juan-les-Pins 1925, Villa Belle-Rose, 20 août 1925," and on the last page, "Juan-les-Pins, 13 septembre 1925." The gap in the dates between the end of the one and the beginning of the other may suggest a temporary absence from Juan-les-Pins between the 1st and the 20th of August.

And what an amazing number of "double images" and portraits of young women strongly resembling Marie-Thérèse there are in Carnet No.88! These are undoubtedly preparatory sketches for *Les Modistes* (Fig.50), *La Statuaire* (Fig.55), *Woman with Mandolin* (July 1925) and *Painter and Model* (Z-VII-30, 1926) . This trend continues in the Parisian Carnet No.89, of October, November, and December 1925.

In Carnet No.90, from December 1925 to 21 March 1926, there is a profusion of "sculptural sketches" and "double images," many relating to *The Seated Girl* 1926 (Fig.4), and "Sculptural Sketches" (Fig.5). One representation in particular is of superb execution and sensitivity of line, and is most beautiful and revealing. In it, within the striking likeness of Marie-Thérèse, the features of Picasso's face are clearly discernible in a "double image" (Fig.26), while the flowing outline of a girl's body graces what appears to be Picasso's old fireside armchair (Fig.35).

---

[78]   GLIMCHER (ed.) *supra* note 39 p.324

[79]   GLIMCHER (ed.), *supra* note 39, p.325

The place and date on the last page of Carnet No.88-Juan-les-Pins, 13 Septembre 1925- suggests that Picasso returned to Paris from Juan-les-Pins around the middle of September. He brought with him a large number of sketches and canvases of still lifes which he continued to work on in his atelier. Among them is one, in green and blue, containing the hidden, nude, form of Marie-Thérèse (Z-V-416, 1925). It is described by Daix. If we accept as correct the dating of it by Zervos, who places it at the end of 1925 in his catalogue, and if we note its similarity to another still life, this one in earth tones (Z-VII-3, 1926) and dated by Zervos's catalogue to the beginning of 1926 then the still life with the nude body of Marie-Thérèse was probably done, not long after Picasso's return from Juan-les-Pins.

If this was Picasso's first representation of Marie-Thérèse nude, it confirms her assertion that their intimacy did not commence until Picasso painted her in the nude, several months after the first meeting.

Conclusion

A large body of Picasso's work dated to November 1925 gives clear indication of increasing intimacy. I refer here again to *Le Couple Amoureux* and *Le Couple dans l'Herbe* (Fig.47 and 49), Picasso's most tender and loving sketches, reflecting his identification with Manet, who like Picasso had accosted a young girl in Paris; the "coded" but unmistakable initials of Marie-Thérèse in the *Musical Instrument* (Fig.44); the litho of a young girl who strikingly resembles Marie-Thérèse (Fig.25), and a sketch in Carnet No.90 for November 1925.

Picasso's first visit to Émilie Marguerite's villa probably took place in October or November 1925, when Marie-Thérèse was down with a cold.

Picasso got the inspiration for *Les Modistes* at 6 cité d'Alfort towards the end of 1925, possibly in December, when Marie-Thérèse's sister, who was a student, would have been there for the Christmas holidays, and he finished the work early in January 1926.

From 1926 there is an explosion in the number of images of Marie-Thérèse in Picasso's *oeuvre*.

It is tremendously important to realize to what an extent Picasso was inspired by his youthful muse long before January 1927! From 1925, a considerable body of his monumental work was directly related to Marie-Thérèse, and later it included her beautiful sister and other members of the Walter family.

Picasso has also made a number of highly important symbolic references to his state of frustration in 1925, when he was unable to possess Marie-Thérèse.   All the Picassos of those years containing references to Marie-Thérèse and hitherto unexplained, must be seen in the light of a much earlier entry into his life by her than he had stated to Gilot.

The question remains unanswered whether Picasso had Marie-Thérèse with him during his sojourn at Juan-les-Pins in 1926. Does it matter? The "Bearded Painter's Saga" in the Juan-les-Pins Carnet of that year is a continuation of Picasso's expression of personal conflicts and drama, an expression that in 1925 had produced *The Cage* (Fig.53), *The Studio with the Plaster Head* (Fig.54), *La Statuaire* (Fig.55), *The Embrace* (Fig.56) and others at a time when Picasso was still torn between his duty towards Olga and his overpowering desire for Marie-Thérèse. In the end there is no love greater than forbidden love, and so the Picassian epic of "The Bearded Painter's Saga" comes to a predictable climax:

> Picasso confronts Olga, questions her authority, and finally wrenches it away from her. The scene is represented symbolically by the Bearded Painter's taking the cane into his own hands and, with the voluptuous "Femme Enfant" at his side, leaving Olga to become once more the master of his own life. (Fig.14)

What followed this liberation is well known in the history of art and is of no concern here.

It was the enigmatic *Seated Girl*, the subject of which bore a striking resemblance to Marie-Thérèse even though the work was dated by Picasso "1926," that stimulated my interest in the relationship between the middle-aged artist and the teen-aged "Femme-Enfant." And as I searched for the artist I discovered the man, with all his joys, his heartbreaks, and his fears. The distant and unknown past slowly revealed the villa at 6 cité d'Alfort, a place never once mentioned in the numerous monographs on Picasso. Yet Picasso visited it frequently during several years, had a Studio there, and made it the background for one of his greatest curvilinear paintings *Les Modistes* of 1926!

> Picasso the man kept this villa a well-guarded secret from all but Picasso the artist, who was a compulsive raconteur of all that the man felt and did, and he scrupulously recorded and dated all that the man felt about and did with its youngest inhabitant in works like *The Seated Girl...*
>
> The dates Picasso put on his works during this time were the true ones, and only twice did he change the name of the location of a work: "Paris" October 1935 instead of Boulogne (Fig.18), and again "Paris" instead of Juan-les-Pins, Z-VIII-278 1936. The paintings done at Maisons Alfort were said to have been done in Paris, but that place was a suburb of Paris.

In looking into the early relations between Picasso and Marie-Thérèse, I set myself the arduous tasks of establishing the chronology of countless paintings and sketches, of observing, comparing, and interpreting those works, and also of acquiring the insight into Picasso, an insight obtained over the years from his most intimate friends. Finally by bringing together my knowledge of the man and his works, the many seemingly isolated fragments of information fitted together like pieces in a gigantic jigsaw puzzle, and it spoke to me directly:

> "...it is not sufficient to know an artist's works; it is also necessary to know when he did them, why, how, under what circumstances... Someday there will undoubtedly be a science, it may be called the science of man, which will seek to learn more about man in general through the study of creative man. I often think about

such a science, and I want to leave to posterity a documentation that will be as complete as possible. That is why I put a date on everything I do..."[80] [81]

During this study, I trailed Picasso closely, and it became obvious to me that art is not a configuration of forms, or a sequence of schools and styles, that one can analyze with a distant and objective academic eye. Art is the science of man, the whole man, with all of his strengths and failings, reflecting his background, his beliefs, and his endeavours.

With Picasso art has always been the study of man and nothing else. Influenced by the Surrealist credo that all passion leading to sexual exultation was a positive good not to be denied by taboos, bewitched by Marie-Thérèse, Picasso embarked in an *amour fou* with this Woman-Child and acted out his passion, his fantasies, and his dramas. But, characteristically, Picasso was more interested in the artistic portrayal of his feelings than in acting them out, and this necessity to record his emotions became instrumental in directing me to the discovery that he had met Marie-Thérèse Walter much earlier than hitherto believed or than he himself wanted to acknowledge.

Jean Cocteau's, "I am a lie that always tells the truth", uniquely applies to Picasso within the context of this work.

---

[80]   Picasso to Brassai, recorded in G. BRASSAI, *Conversations avec Picasso*, Paris, Gallimard, 1943.

[81]   See photo 5 by André VILLERS, *Dos d'une toile de Picasso*.

155

Photo 5 *Dos d'une toile de Picasso.*
    André Villers, Mougins.

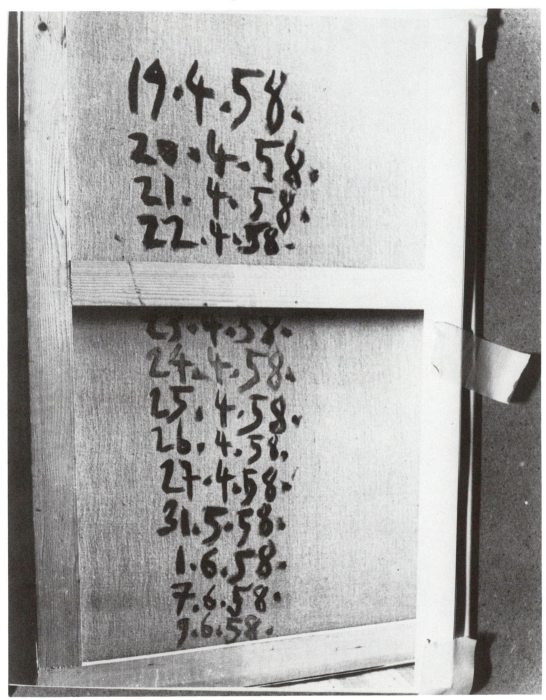

Addendum

On November 28th 1986, after completing the first draft of this study, I had an opportunity to peruse a remarkable and totally unknown collection of drawings and pen and ink sketches by Picasso that the artist had given to one of his close female friends. Among these sketches were a number of first state lithos including *Woman's Head* of November 1925 (Fig.25 in our study); it was dedicated by Picasso to his friend.

When asked, "Who is that girl in the lithograph?", the woman replied without hesitation, "But this is Marie-Thérèse of course! <u>Picasso told me so,</u> and the people who knew Marie-Thérèse well, recognized her from it".

As close as this woman was to Picasso, she was unaware of the lithograph's date.

Acknowledgements

1-   It was my chance encounter with Marie-Thérèse Walter, shortly after Picasso's death, that catalyzed my intuitive thought processes, readiness, and drive forcing me to follow this inquiry when confronted with *The Seated Girl*. If by exploding the Picassian myth that she and Picasso did not meet until 1927 I am exposing Marie-Thérèse herself, then so be it. I do it with a clear conscience, for payment of tribute to Picasso's youthful Muse is long overdue.

2-   I wish to give my special thanks to the relatives of Émilie Marguerite and to those on the paternal side of Marie-Thérèse's family, who kindly opened doors onto the past by assisting with my personal inquiries, and those relating to the Walter family.

3-   I am grateful as well to that dedicated Picasso scholar, Josep Palau i Fabre, for his long and fascinating discourses on Picasso's complexity (Barcelona 1984 and 1985). The added insight he gave me, allowed me to make a more penetrating assessment of Picasso's relations with Marie-Thérèse, than would otherwise have been possible.

4-   To Dr. Jean Sutherland Boggs, my thanks for words of encouragement, and advice concerning *The Seated Woman*

1926-1927, Art Gallery of Ontario Coll., and to Brydon Smith, Associate Director, Research and Collections, National Gallery of Canada, I owe a vote of gratitude for his pertinent observation relating to Picasso's "double image" in *The Seated Woman*, 1926-1927.

5-   To Denys Sutton Esq. I express thanks for his interest in "Picasso and Marie-Thérèse, 1925-1927", and for moral support given to a Physician poaching in the preserve of the art historians.

6-   To Dr. James Lambert, biographer and historian, Laval University, Québec City, my grateful thanks for the long hours he spent in editing the manuscript, and for his critical assessment of it.

7-   To the "Maître" Marie-Claude, my wife, whose charm and expert legal knowledge made possible the second part of this study, in France.

8-   Finally, anonymity is all too often the price of disclosure, and since some of this research involved off the record discussions, acknowledgement by name of all my sources is unfortunately not possible.

Table of Contents

Figures

Photos